LANTRY

". . . War *IS* Declared!
I know now why I was born back up
out of the earth! It's William Lantry
against the whole vampire-disbelieving, body-burning,
graveyard-annihilating world.
So, you there, city, people, customs,
clean minds in clean bodies.
You who cannot, *must* not, believe in me.
Death has returned to your world.
I will make more dead ones, more companions,
so I won't be alone and lonely . . . NOW!"

PILLAR OF FIRE
RAY BRADBURY

Pillar of Fire

and Other Plays

for today, tomorrow, and beyond tomorrow

by Ray Bradbury

RLI: VLM 7 (VLR 5–8)
IL 7–adult

PILLAR OF FIRE AND OTHER PLAYS
A Bantam Book / November 1975

Published simultaneously in the United States and Canada

Bantam Books are published by Bantam Books, Inc. Its trademark, consisting of the words "Bantam Books" and the portrayal of a bantam, is registered in the United States Patent Office and in other countries. Marca Registrada. Bantam Books, Inc., 666 Fifth Avenue, New York, New York 10019.

PRINTED IN THE UNITED STATES OF AMERICA

Contents

Introduction

This book is dedicted to Kirk Mee, the first director to produce *Pillar of Fire*. His imagination brought the play to life with incredible intensity. His theatrical knowledge enabled me to cut and revise the play for its own benefit.

Kirk Mee is a proper way to start, for he taught me some of the old truths all over again. The best one being: simplicity is the soul of drama production. I have seen too many plays founder and roll on their sides when overproduced, overdressed, overstaged. When in doubt, strip away, lower your voice, stand in center stage with one light, and do the play. Better no sets than too many. Better one candle than a battery of glare. Better a whisper than all the fake sounds of all the fake rock artists in modern times.

There are exceptions to this, of course, but so rare as to have little bearing on my preface here.

Let me give an example of the sort of trouble you get into if you try to overproduce the plays in this book.

Some years back I put my two-act comedy *The Anthem Sprinters* in rehearsal here in Los Angeles, with my commendable director Charles Rome Smith, and as fine a cast of Irish/Scotch/Welsh actors as ever fell into a pub and poured out the other side. Since we had no money with which to put on the play, they gave me their lives three or four nights a week for a year. We celebrated our first anniversary as a "family" long before we got enough money to stage the comedy. During that year I wrote and rewrote yet again the long play, and, on occasion, we staged it at small drama societies around town. We liked what we saw. We liked what we felt about the play.

Then we made a dire mistake. We found some money. Some was in my pockets. Some was in the pockets of a man who haplessly wandered into our rehearsal one night. We rented the Coronet Theatre and first off built us a bog. Now why I ever let my producer convince me that we could *use* a bog, I cannot say. It is all lost in fog and mist back there in time. I went along with it, anyway, for the producer said we needed the blamed thing for my army of Sprinters to trudge through, philosophising about the dirth of sex and the squander of rain.

No sooner was the bog built than the play sank. Which is to say every time our actors climbed up and down around the rear of the stage where the bog was waiting for them, their voices were swallowed by space and went down without a trace.

"Speak up!" I yelled, on occasion, breaking a vow of silence I have kept pretty faithfully in connection with my actors and my director.

Speak up they did, but to little effect. The bog was too far back and their yelling spoiled what their philosophy was about.

"My God," I said to my director and producer, "let's get them out of that bog. March them down into the audience and around in front of the stage apron. Let the area just in front of the audience be the bog. *That* way we can at least hear the lines."

"That bog cost us five thousand dollars, we *got* to use it!" cried my producer.

"It may have cost us five thousand dollars, but

right now it is costing us the entire play. If you can't hear the lines, you don't stay awake. And I'll be blasted if I'll stage a comedy for a company of sleepers. To hell with the bog, to hell with the five thousand dollars. Get those actors out of stage rear and up stage front! Try it!"

We tried it. It worked.

The actors marched around in the audience and the bog was there, by magic, simply because it didn't exist, but *did* exist in the language spoken.

So when the curtain went up on opening night, we still had that five thousand dollar bog waiting at stage rear. Everyone could see it. But no one ever used it, save for a fast exit or a nice quick entrance.

I should have seen the problem before we spent the money.

I give you the same advice about the plays you hold here in your hands. Don't spend money, spend imagination. There is no reason to overdress or overproduce these texts. All three plays can be done without sets, with rear-projection, on occasion, if you wish, but don't let it worry you. Build me no bogs; when you sink out of sight I won't be able to help you.

How did these plays *happen* to me?

The Fog Horn resulted from an encounter I had one night with the tumbled ruins of the Venice Pier and the gigantic roller-coaster tracks and ties lying in the sand. Looking at them I said, "What's this dinosaur doing lying on the shore, why did it come here?" Two nights later I awoke hearing the fog horn blowing and blowing far down the coast. "Of course!" I thought. "The fog horn! It sounds like an animal. *It* called that dinosaur in to the shore!"

I jumped out of bed and wrote *The Fog Horn* in a few hours.

Pillar of Fire was caused by the quasi-intellectuals

who mob through our society bullying us about our tastes, telling us that comic-strip cartoon books are bad for our digestion, worse for our imagination, and so should be burned. I would gladly Gunpowder Plot these ignorant social reformers out of existence, at least in my stories, and so set out in a fine rage to erase them with a large India rubber eraser.

Kaleidoscope was a word-association test I tried twenty-five years ago to see how terrified I might be if I threw myself down an elevator shaft.

If I were to further describe the essence of these three plays, how would I describe them?

Well, *The Fog Horn* is a poetic dialogue, really, isn't it, about Loneliness and Time and strangely unrequited love? I didn't know this at the time I wrote it, but that's how it turned out. A fine lovely sad Surprise.

Pillar of Fire? One can best explain it as the drama of a sympathetic madman enveloped and finally destroyed by his obsession. This story, this character, this play, I see now, were rehearsals for my later novel and film *Fahrenheit 451*. If Montag is a burner of books who wakens to reading and becomes obsessed with saving mind-as-printed-upon-matter, then Lantry is the books themselves, he is the thing to be saved. In an ideal world, he and Montag would have met, set up shop and lived happily ever after: library and saver of libraries, book and reader, idea and flesh to preserve the idea.

So you play Lantry as pure paranoia. You play him like a whole library run amok because it knows, and we know, that unless it runs fast with Lantry's legs, it will be put to the torch and carried off in smoke. Lantry's family is all of the dark/bright lovely/horrible books ever written. If he had any childhood at all, he was Quasimodo aged three. If he had middle years, they were Jekyll and Hyde. If ever he loved it was behind the mask of the Phantom of the Opera in Paris.

You play the obsessions then, and whatever image and metaphor come to hand. You play the passion to survive. Lantry is every library that we ever loved and hated to leave when someone whispered "closing time" and the green-shaded lamps dimmed and we had to shut our books and creep on mouse-feet home. That love, turned to despair at saving the love, inhabits *Pillar of Fire*.

And what inhabits *Kaleidoscope?* Panic and terror and sadness, with a touch of beauty. One day twenty-five years ago I turned a bunch of men out, upside down, into space, to see what horrors and delights I might find with men so abandoned and so turned. What if, I asked myself, one night you fell downstairs into your basement but the stairs never ended, the basement had no bottom, and you kept falling forever?

In this last play then, what you enact is panic and exhilaration, terror and self-revelation; that moment when each man, alone, falling, dredges up what pitiful ounce of philosophy he has in the bin to help him through a night that, no matter what he does, will never end.

What you have in most of my stories and plays then is rarely a highly individualized character (I blunder into these on occasion) but Ideas grown super outsize; Ideas that sieze people and change them forever. So, I should imagine, in order to do my plays at all, you must become the Idea, the Idea that destroys, or the Idea that prevails.

Whether or not you can cram a dinosaur into a theatre, I do not know. You must try. And one of the ways of trying of course, along with the aid of a good sound track and fine lighting, is to let the Idea of Loneliness itself invade your very bones so that you become Loneliness, the Night, the horn crying out, and the Beast come searching to see, find, know, and turn away to go lose himself in another billion years of loveless sleep.

So it follows that the actors in my plays instead of playing character in the old fashioned or accepted sense must become, if you wish, a purer, or at least a different thing: an Idea in motion, a passion on its way to destruction or survival, a love lost or kept, a panic continuing until death shuts it off.

Costumes for the plays must be, and are, simple.

The two characters in *The Fog Horn* can be dressed in ordinary work shirts and pants, with a seaman's cap, perhaps, for the older man.

The merest skeleton of a set will do. Build a slight, circular rise in mid-stage down front, with a rail to hold onto, as the two men pace and speak, looking out at the audience as if the audience were the night-sea itself. The rest is darkness, spot-lighting, and the sounds of sea, horn, and beast.

Pillar of Fire's problems are few. Lantry should appear in a dark suit, greened with age; some ancient dinner attire, perhaps, badly spoiled by time. The rest of the cast should wear dark jumpsuits or body stockings, cheaply purchased. In the Hearth scenes, the performers should be draped in sun-colored, orange colored scarves, and the man in charge of the Hearth itself should be uniformed brightly, to reflect the burning optimism of that place. Beyond that, where indicated, the play needs few props, a decent soundtrack to let us hear the huge whisper of the Hearth, a few good bars from a sombre and then a heartier Bach, and imaginative lighting on an almost empty stage. Two coffins should be available, one very dark and of no particular singularity for Lantry to come out of. The other, utilized later in the Hearth, should be as bright and fantastically painted as an Egyptian sarcophagus, the sun-symbol being repeated a dozen times or more upon its surfaces. The Hearth itself can be a brightly illuminated red maw at stage rear. Borrow one of those roller-rung-ball-bearing ladders from a van-and-storage truck to put your coffins on. When it comes time to slide them into the Hearth, they shoot along splendidly on the swift rolling rungs, and vanish into the "fire" with a grand effect.

Kaleidoscope, it can be seen immediately, could be staged thirty different ways, from Peter Pan grandiloquent, with invisible wires and flying harnesses costing thousands, down to Simple Simon poor, which means standing three or four actors on one level, with others on tables or step-ladders or risers painted black against an all black background behind them. Variations on this might be large black wheels spotted here and there about the stage, to which the actors might cling to be turned roundabout upside down at various times during the play.

But something like an immense book-shelf, or series of shelves, painted black, could be knocked together cheaply for your best effect. The actors could lie flat out on this, with their heads toward the audience, speaking their lines. Then if you wish an effect of men briefly spinning in space the actors could achieve this by just rolling on their sides or over on their backs. In this fashion, the actor would be in complete control of his actions at all times. The entire crew, arranged at various levels on such a large, dark, and therefore invisible book-case, would surely suggest the Space that we utilize in the play. Stars could be projected all about them without necessarily revealing the construction you have put up.

The children need not appear at the end of this play. Their voices could be heard as the small trace of fire moves across the night sky.

There. I have said enough, no, more than enough about these plays.

Run grab them. Do them with great zest and fine gusto. Celebrate their terrors and delights. Get you to New England's coast, Poe's fiery tomb, and all of universal Space.

But . . . a last reminder.

Build me no Bogs!

Ray Bradbury
Los Angeles, California
Spring, 1975

Pillar of Fire

At rise of curtain, darkness. Shadow shapes of tombstones here and there (projected), but in the main, darkness. We make out a coffin disposed alone amidst the graves. The lid opens slowly. We see only a hand. After a long moment, a very pale man in a dark suit sits up, slowly, achingly, half-blinded by sleep or that which is deeper than sleep. He feels himself. He climbs from the coffin and looks about, stunned.

LANTRY

I am dead. But . . . I am not dead.

He is examining himself incredulously.

LANTRY

I am reborn. In what place, to what time, for what reason?

His hand falls upon a tombstone, which he sees.

LANTRY

Wait. . . . Lantry? Yes . . . William Lantry. My name! Why? Lord, *someone* speak! Tell me! (*He almost weeps.*)

Voices approach. He pulls back in shadow.

Two men enter in dark jumpsuits, with a single symbol of fire on their breast-fronts. They carry spades and some peculiar kind of laser device, and are immaculate for all their being workers.

SMITH

Come on, Harry, this is it.

HARRY
They been waiting hundreds of years. Another ten seconds won't sweat them.

SMITH
This is special, though, this grave, this is history. I mean there should be newspapers here, television, radio. Photographers should take pictures! Listen, this is the *very last one*. In all the world, Harry, there are no more dead people! In all this country and all the countries of the world at long last there are no dead, no bodies, no corpses, no cemeteries, no graveyards. Think of it!

HARRY (*sits on coffin*)
I'm thinking.

SMITH
That's your trouble. Nothing gets through to you. We've finally *done* it! Cleaned the earth, tidied up the soil, cleansed mankind of flesh and bones, of ribs and skulls. All gone except . . . er . . . Lazarus here. (*Nods to box.*)

LANTRY (*aside*)
Lazarus . . . yes, Lazarus, *that's* my name. Called forth from the tomb, to do . . . *what?*

SMITH
A historic occasion, Harry! Celebrate!

HARRY (*dryly; waves hand weakly*)
Hurrah.

SMITH (*peering at coffin lid*)
What's *this* one's name again?

HARRY (*without looking, rises*)
Plumtree.

LANTRY (*sotto voce; angry at this*)
Lantry! Lantry!

SMITH
Well, good soul, lone Christian or whatever, he's the last dead 'un in history, the last actual flesh-and-blood corpse lying in the ground. He is extra-special. In a way he should be put in a museum like a mummy. (*Bends, opens coffin lid.*) Hold on . . . ! We didn't *finish* last night, did we?

HARRY
No.

SMITH
There *was* one more coffin, wasn't there?

HARRY
Yes.

SMITH (*peering*)
It's empty!

HARRY
You've got the wrong hole . . . here . . . (*Reads tombstone.*) L-a-n-t—Lantry.

SMITH
You see? That's him. He's gone. And his body was here last night.

HARRY
We can't be sure. We didn't look.

SMITH
People don't bury empty coffins. He was in his box. Now he isn't. Smell that smell? He was here, all right.

HARRY
Nobody would have taken the body, would they?

SMITH
What for?

HARRY
A curiosity, perhaps? He was *special*, eh?

SMITH (*almost as if by rote, mechanically*)
Don't be ridiculous. People just don't steal. Nobody steals. *Nobody* steals.

HARRY
Well, then, there's only one solution.

SMITH
And?

HARRY
He got up and walked away. Yes. That's it. He *got up* and *walked away!* (*Beams at his own joke.*)

SMITH
Harry, we're in big *trouble*. What will the Officials say if we show up empty-handed?

A siren wails, interrupting. A light flares on the sky. They turn and look and blink.

SMITH
There goes Lazarus-But-One. Into the old Fire. So long. Good-bye.

LANTRY (*sotto voce; aside; moves off, afraid*)
The incinerator! That *Fire!*

SMITH
Good old Fire Place, Fine Hearth, great bonfire. I wish *I'd* thought of that, Harry.

HARRY
What, the Incinerator?

SMITH
Death pays fine cash, son. The man who built the first one, a millionaire. And all the rest since. Every city, town, village, you name it. They all got an official and therefore special Holy Incinerator. Where we all wind up.

HARRY
You before me, sir.

LANTRY (*aside*)
The Incinerator. That light on the hill. Yes, yes. In the town a man dies. No sooner is he cold than his relatives pack him into a car and drive him swiftly to—

HARRY
The Incinerator. You're right. We grew up as Diggers. *Should* have been Officials. Hey, what do we do after tonight? Why . . . we're . . .

SMITH
Out of work. True. Out of work.

LANTRY (*slowly inspired, but still unsure; aside*)
Not if I have anything to say about it.

HARRY (*shrugs; a beat*)
You ever been inside the Incinerator?

SMITH (*snorts*)
Sure! Haven't *you*?

HARRY
I never knew anyone *died. Yet.*

SMITH
Oh, it's a beautiful place. Gorgeous. You *must* see it!

HARRY
I will, soon enough.

They bend to hoist the coffin.

LANTRY (*picking it up; aside*)
Soon enough.

LANTRY steps forward into the light.

LANTRY
Gentlemen! I bid you welcome!

Startled, they let the coffin fall.

HARRY
Hey, what are you doing here?

SMITH
Ah, shut up, Harry.

HARRY
How'd you *get* here?

SMITH
Harry. (*A beat.*) Sir, this is off-limits. No citizens allowed. You know the law.

LANTRY
I know the law.

SMITH
Well, then . . .

LANTRY
You're looking for a body?

SMITH
That's none of your affair.

HARRY
No, none!

LANTRY
I think I know where it is. I took it.

SMITH (*stunned*)
You . . . *took* it?

HARRY
You got no right! How dare—

LANTRY
The right of first possession. It belongs to me.

HARRY (*pulls out pad and pencil*)
All right. Let's just have your name for the Authorities!

LANTRY
Lantry.

HARRY (*writes, peering at pad; spells*)
L . . . a . . . n . . .

He freezes. LANTRY finishes it for him.

LANTRY
. . . t . . . r . . . y . . . .

HARRY (*stunned*)
It's a joke?

LANTRY shakes his head.

HARRY
Joe, isn't it a joke?

SMITH
A joke, sure, a joke! (*Laughs.*)

LANTRY
Well, you'll get your body, anyway.

SMITH
We will?

HARRY
Where is it?

LANTRY
Here.

He reaches out and strangles HARRY. SMITH watches, fascinated.

SMITH
Here, now, what're you *doing*?

LANTRY
Getting you your body.

SMITH (*still fascinated, curious, watching*)
But that's no way to do it . . . er . . . People don't murder people. Not anymore, they don't.

LANTRY (*holds* HARRY'S *neck firmly*)
They do *again*. There. (*Lets the body fall.*)

SMITH (*bends, peers*)
What's wrong with him? He's not *really* dead? He *can't* be! People don't *do* that!

LANTRY moves calmly to put his hands around Smith's neck now, as Smith continues to comment, by rote, on the rules of this future society, as he is slowly strangled and his voice lessens, and finally he is still.

SMITH (*sagging slowly, eyes wide*)
People don't do that . . . why . . . people don't *do* that. They don't do that . . . they don't do . . . they don't . . .

Silence. LANTRY holds the dead SMITH by his throat a moment longer.

LANTRY
What, not even a groan, a cry for mercy? Dear

me. What will the Officials think? Two bodies instead of one. Ah, well.

He puts SMITH's body in the coffin, then swiftly puts HARRY's body in on top of it and slams the lid.

LANTRY

Peace. (*He turns, paces, eyes the sky, the land.*) Good. Good to walk again. Good to feel the wind and hear the leaves running like mice about my feet. Good to see the cold stars almost blown away in the wind. . . . Good even to know *fear* again. And . . . (*Feels himself.*) . . . I *am* afraid. Oh, yes. The very fact I *move* makes me the Enemy! An Enemy of all mankind. For there is not another friend, another *special* dead man just like me to whom I can turn for help, for consolation. So . . . War *IS* Declared! I know now why I was born back up out of the earth! It's William Lantry against the whole vampire-disbelieving, body-burning, graveyard-annihilating world. So, you there, city, people, customs, clean minds in clean bodies. You who cannot, *must* not, believe in me. Death has returned to your world. I will make more dead ones, more companions, so I won't be alone and lonely. . . . *NOW!*

A young man hurries through, whistling.

LANTRY

Oh . . . *sir!*

The man stops, turns. LANTRY comes forward.

LANTRY

Do you have a match?

The man strikes one into fire. LANTRY looks at it. A beat. Leans forward. Blows it out.

Instant blackout.

In the dark, a grand blast of Bach's Sinfonia from Cantata #29.

The colors change. All sun color now; oranges and yellows permeate the sky, the backdrops, the people. The music flows with summer sounds.

A VOICE (*gently whispering*)
Welcome to the Hearth. Welcome to the Fires of God. Welcome to the place of the Sun. The Fire Place is always open. Summer and winter. Night and day. The Hearth is ready to welcome. The Fire is here to cleanse. The Sun is here to burn and make peace. Welcome, welcome....

Enter AN OLD MAN in colors of sun and summer.

THE OLD MAN
Yes, welcome, welcome, come in, come in. . . . Put on the warm summer colors, brighten yourselves . . . that's it, yes, yes.

For THE OLD MAN is being followed by A YOUNG COUPLE, who are pulling bright-colored capes over their darker clothes. THE OLD MAN helps adjust the capes.

THE YOUNG WOMAN
We've been waiting so long.

THE YOUNG MAN
So long.

THE OLD MAN
Well, then, twice welcome. Put on summer, sir, put on summer.

He hands him a bright orange scarf to drape across his shoulders. An immense whispering sounds now.

THE YOUNG MAN (*listens, curious*)
What's *that?*

THE OLD MAN (*listens, laughs*)
That? Why, the fire, of course. The fire that rushes up the high round flue . . . the fire that burns all night, all day, forever, beyond that wall, within those stones, the fire, the sun, or the brother of the sun, you might say, a friend to all of us. (*Moves; points.*) Come into the bakery. Feel how warm. It's summer here all year. And the music? Have you *truly* listened?

They all listen to the heavenly spheres in transit about them on the air.

THE OLD MAN
Bach rejuvenated! Bach made more alive than he ever hoped or dreamed! Not music of death, but music of life and fire, of all June, July, August, put away in sweetest energies and flame. I—

A bell sounds. THE OLD MAN shuts up, turns.

THE OLD MAN
Hist! Watch. And know Joy!

The music rises. LANTRY appears, surprised.

THE OLD MAN
Oh, dear! Sir, sir, stand away. I mean . . . oh, welcome . . . but . . . stand back! The Procession of Joy begins!

LANTRY
The procession . . . ?

THE OLD MAN
Of Joy, of Joy! Wear summer, sir, put summer on. Here.

He gives and arranges the sun-colored scarf upon LANTRY's shoulders, then pulls him aside and nods.

THE OLD MAN
Music, begin again. Sound of children *arise*. And now, the procession!

During the above, the music rises, the sounds of children laughing, play all about.

LANTRY and the others stand waiting, intensely curious.

THE OLD MAN gestures, for the procession is obviously late.

THE OLD MAN
The *Procession!*

In rolls a golden box on golden wheels, all to itself. The box is covered with sun symbols.

The box rolls to a slow halt, then creeps by at a snail's pace.

LANTRY (*stunned*)
That is . . . a . . . *procession?*

THE OLD MAN
Yes! A procession through summer to the Sun!

LANTRY
And what's inside the coffin?

THE OLD MAN (*shocked*)
Coffin? No, no. Sir, surely you know better.

LANTRY
Sorry . . .

For THE YOUNG COUPLE are muttering, discontented, their faces shadowed.

THE OLD MAN
This is the Hearthing Place.

LANTRY (*going along with it*)
Of course, how silly of me!

THE OLD MAN
Which transfers souls to the New Life Beyond.

LANTRY
How *could* I have forgotten!

THE COUPLE are smiling again. THE OLD MAN is satisfied.

THE OLD MAN
In procession now. We shall accompany the exuberant soul of Minnie Davis Hopkins to the Hearth.

THE COUPLE fall in behind the golden box. LANTRY moves into place, steered by THE OLD MAN.

LANTRY (*to the couple; nods to the box*)
Someone you know?

THE YOUNG WOMAN (*offended*)
His mother!

THE YOUNG MAN
My *mother!*

LANTRY
Sorry . . .

THE YOUNG MAN
Nothing to be sorry about. I wish I were her, and knew Joy.

LANTRY (*dryly*)
Perhaps I can *arrange* it . . . ?

THE YOUNG MAN
What?

LANTRY (*shrugs; stands away*)
Move along to Joy.

THE OLD MAN
Yes, on to Happiness! So! . . . So! Music. Laughter.
Oh, hear the children of Time!

Music, much childish laughter. The organ music rises.

The light grows more intensely yellow. Suns appear everywhere on the backdrops. The box stops where the greatest sun-symbol fire-image burns toward the back of the area. THE OLD MAN takes hold of one edge of the box.

THE OLD MAN
Minnie Davis Hopkins, who *still* lives, live only *more!*

THE YOUNG MAN and WOMAN hold the other corners, wait. They frown at LANTRY. He steps to hold the fourth corner.

THE OLD MAN
You that were born of the Sun, return to the Sun!

The fire roars higher, as they stroke the bright box.

THE OLD MAN
To live is a sweet burning,
To die is not to die,
But live in flame forever
And with God occupy
The time that's left for burning,
A billion years to sup!
So open wide God's laughter,
And let Him eat you up!

They tilt the carrier. The box slides off and down away, gone out of sight. An immense flux of flaming roar, as of a rocket almost, taking off! Music. Mixtures of children's laughter. The light fades.

THE OLD MAN beams, smiles, shakes his head, pats one and all.

THE YOUNG MAN and YOUNG WOMAN smile and shake his hand, and turn to shake LANTRY's hand, but he is turned away, vastly puzzled and disturbed. They exit, leaving THE OLD MAN with LANTRY.

THE OLD MAN (*gestures to the fire*)
It burns ceaselessly, a solid golden river flowing up out of the earth toward the sky. Anything you launch on the river is borne upward, vanishing, forever!

LANTRY (*turned away; dryly*)
You *do* go on.

LANTRY turns and goes to look at the singing fires.

THE OLD MAN
Is anything . . . er . . . *wrong?*

LANTRY
Wrong? How can anything be wrong in such a perfect world?

THE OLD MAN
True. (*Muses.*) When were you here last?

LANTRY
Never.

THE OLD MAN
Never?

LANTRY
Never in my life.

THE OLD MAN
But that's impossible. (*Thinks.*) *Isn't* it?

LANTRY
I exaggerate. I was here as a boy. But one forgets.

THE OLD MAN (*still not convinced; his face darker*)
I shall be pleased to guide you on a tour.

LANTRY
No, no, thanks. Let me explain.
No one in my family has died since I was a child.
That's why—

THE OLD MAN
You have used the word "died," sir. We do *not* use that word!

LANTRY (*laughs, trying to make a joke of it*)
We all have to die sometime.

THE OLD MAN (*steps farther back*)
We do not, sir! Nothing ends, everything goes on, forever. Nothing spoils, nothing stops.

LANTRY
Have you never left a pound of cheese out in the sun?

THE OLD MAN
Sir!

LANTRY
Sorry.

THE OLD MAN
Sorry? (*starts off, turns, thinks*) But, then, oh yes. You *must* be one of those just returned from Mars . . . ?

LANTRY
Mars?

THE OLD MAN (*trying to convince himself, baffled*)
Born and raised there? Used to *their* dread customs? People *do* die *there*. People *are* buried there? Things *do* spoil . . . on *Mars.*

LANTRY (*saved, and making use of it*)
Yes, Mars, that's it!

THE OLD MAN
Which Apollo flight did you return on?

LANTRY
Why . . . the most recent.

THE OLD MAN (*not satisfied, suddenly wary*)
And that would be . . . ?

LANTRY (*impulsively*)
Last *month!*

THE OLD MAN (*suspicious now*)
I see. (*Turns to go.*)

LANTRY
No, you don't see—wait!

THE OLD MAN (*turning back*)
For what, sir?

LANTRY
You say nothing dies, nothing ends, nothing spoils?

THE OLD MAN
I do not say that, sir, the Program says it.

LANTRY
Then you are not afraid of ends, of finishes, of darkness.

THE OLD MAN
I look into the sun, sir, and am not blind.

LANTRY
Look further, then.

He has reached THE OLD MAN and now takes hold of his throat.

LANTRY
What do you see?

THE OLD MAN
Gah!

LANTRY (*insists, wild*)
What do you *see?*

THE OLD MAN
Oh no, no, save me! *Darkness!* (*Dies.*)

LANTRY
You have passed the test, sir. The answer is correct.

He turns swiftly to haul the body to the carrier. As he deposits it, the music rises.

LANTRY (*inspired; calls out commands*)
Music! Yes! Laughter of children! More, more! No, no, not *happy* laughter. Laughter that is somewhat . . . mad! Machines, do you hear? Leaning toward . . . *madness?*

The laughter changes, the light grows more somber.

LANTRY
How fine! Machines that listen and *obey!* Yes, *yes!*

The light is all earth colors now, and dusk. The laughter and music rise to insanity.

LANTRY
Man, born out of darkness, *return* to darkness.

He dumps the body. Organ tones: Bach, long after midnight.

LANTRY starts to run out, stops, feels himself.

LANTRY
Oh, this is . . . *fun!*

A WOMAN ATTENDANT enters abruptly.

THE ATTENDANT (*looks about*)
Was there a service held just now?

LANTRY
There was.

THE ATTENDANT (*takes out pad*)
There was one scheduled for ten o'clock . . . over, done. But it's ten *fifteen* now.

LANTRY
So it is.

THE ATTENDANT (*looks up sharply*)
Who are you?

LANTRY
A fool full of wrong answers, who makes old men suspicious. Everyone *knows* mobs of children are brought here every year of their lives to teach them that fire is fine, going away is sunlight, leaving forever is flame, right?

THE ATTENDANT
I—

LANTRY
Right! But did I *say* any of those things? No. I said darkness, I said die, I said death.

THE ATTENDANT (*stunned and disgusted*)
Unutterable, oh, most unutterable!

LANTRY
Isn't it? Darkness, die, death.

THE ATTENDANT
No, no! (*Puts hands to ears.*)

LANTRY
I'm done.

THE ATTENDANT
No!

LANTRY
I said I'm done.

THE ATTENDANT takes her hands from her ears.

THE ATTENDANT (*sniffs*)
Wha . . . what's that smell?

LANTRY
Smell?

THE ATTENDANT
I walked in the fields once at dusk. That is the smell of . . . earth.

LANTRY (*nods, smiles*)
Earth!

THE ATTENDANT
But, *more* . . . in the field, I found . . . a cow . . . a cow that had expired. A cow that had fallen away to eternity, but lay in the field for . . . a *week.* The smell, oh, the smell! And now . . . it's *here.*

LANTRY
Here. (*Holds out his hand.*)

THE ATTENDANT (*widens her eyes, sniffs*)
You're so . . . pale.

LANTRY
Pale? (*Looks at hand.*) Yes, I never thought.

THE ATTENDANT (*as if reciting catechism*)
People aren't pale. People are tan, sunburned, golden, brown.

LANTRY
People are, yes. But not the dead.

THE ATTENDANT (*motionless*)
Dead?

LANTRY (*produces knife*)
Do you know what this is?

THE ATTENDANT
A knife.

LANTRY
What would you say if I told you I was going to push it straight on into your chest?

THE ATTENDANT
People don't do that . . . people don't do that, people don't—

LANTRY
Yes.

THE ATTENDANT (*by rote*)
You wouldn't do that, you wouldn't . . .

LANTRY (*touches her on her shoulder with knife*)
Yes.

THE ATTENDANT (*reciting catechism*)
People don't kill people. No one kills anyone. No one dies anymore.

LANTRY (*touches her on her brow*)
I just killed your friend.

THE ATTENDANT (*by rote*)
People don't kill.

LANTRY (*touches her on her chest*)
Yours will be the fourth murder in as few hours in the past one hundred years.

THE ATTENDANT (*by rote, as if spelled*)
I'm not going to be killed. I'm not going to be killed.

LANTRY
You're going to stand right there like a hypnotized chicken while I walk around you . . . (*Walks.*) . . . so. And now reach out with this knife.

THE ATTENDANT
You're not reaching out. People don't kill.

LANTRY
To shove in the blade.

THE ATTENDANT
It's not going in.

LANTRY
Die.

THE ATTENDANT
I'm not dying . . . I'm . . .

Her eyes shut. LANTRY catches her as she falls.

Darkness. Instant Bach-at-midnight. A great voice, like LANTRY'S, intones in the dark.

LANTRY'S VOICE
Ashes to ashes, dust to dust.

There is a fantastic explosion, which lights up the night.

LANTRY appears, warms his hands at the sight, holding them out upon the air as the lights rise again.

LANTRY (*wildly to the Universe itself*)
And what was that? Why . . . the Incinerator! The Hearth! The Grand Fire Place! Blown up and making more fire in the hills than all of autumn itself!

A final explosion, a dying of light.

LANTRY
Now, one by one, I'll blow up all the other Incinerator Fire Hearthing Places before anyone suspects they have a man of no ethics whatsoever loose in their midst. Long before they discover that this enemy-variable, this William Lantry, has run amok, I will have torn down and done murder across a world. For I am, after all, invisible. Since crime is impossible in this future world, who dares, who tries to see the obvious beast? (*Holds his hands out . . . gestures. An explosion!*) Delicious!

Blackout.

Lights come up on THREE MEN in dark jumpsuits with bright suns blazoned on the jacket pockets, seated at imaginary computer electronic phone boards. Behind them, vast computer banks and electrical devices are projected on the scrims. There is a hum and moan of machines and soft bells sounding.

A soft bell sounds above the others. One of the OPERATORS pantomimes, palm-printing the air in front of him.

THE OPERATOR (*crisply*)
Central City Data.

LANTRY'S VOICE
Could you give me . . . that is . . . the telephone number of the . . . Police Department?

THE OPERATOR
The what?

LANTRY'S VOICE
Police Department . . . ?

THE OPERATOR (*crisply*)
No such listing!

He "erases" the air with his hand. Disconnect sounds. A second bell rings. The SECOND OPERATOR prints the air with his hand.

SECOND OPERATOR
Central City Data.

LANTRY'S VOICE
Beg pardon, but . . . Police?

SECOND OPERATOR
Sir?

LANTRY'S VOICE
I'm simply trying to find the Police Department!

The FIRST OPERATOR is looking over quizzically at the SECOND, who raises his eyebrows. The FIRST OPERATOR "plugs in," recognizes the voice, listens. The THIRD OPERATOR does the same.

SECOND OPERATOR (*pronouncing it slowly*)
Po-lice. Dee-part—ment?

LANTRY (*guessing*)
Law Enforcement? Law Force?

SECOND OPERATOR
The terms you are using no longer exist, sir.

He gestures. The others begin an electronic track-down.

LANTRY

Sorry, but I don't know—

SECOND OPERATOR

I will connect you with the Peace Control . . . ?

LANTRY

Yes! That's it! Peace! Peace Control!

SECOND OPERATOR

Control it is. One moment.

He "dials" the air, and nods to the THIRD OPERATOR, who nods, winks, "prints" the air with his hand. A bell rings.

THIRD OPERATOR

Peace Control.

LANTRY

Yes, well . . . put me through to Homicide.

THIRD OPERATOR

Sir?

LANTRY

Homicide Division. Investigation of Violence? Assault and Battery? Murder?

THIRD OPERATOR

Sir!

All three OPERATORS are astounded. Their hands work overtime on the air, pantomiming circuit cut-ins.

LANTRY

Is there no department to investigate . . . deaths?

THIRD OPERATOR

Sir, you are in much need of help. (*Checks imaginary circuits on air in front of him.*) You are in a phone station at Salem and Twelfth. Please remain there until the Quiet People arrive.

LANTRY

Quiet people? What! *Quiet* people, did you say?

THIRD OPERATOR

Do not leave that location, sir. Help is on the way.

LANTRY

Sir, sir . . . !

THIRD OPERATOR

Yes?

LANTRY (*takes a deep breath, holds it, explodes*)

Wrong number!

Click-buzz. The system hums, moans. The men gesticulate. All talk into their phones at once.

FIRST OPERATOR

Peace Control, quickly . . . Unit Twelve.

SECOND OPERATOR

Quiet People Unit Seven. . . .

THIRD OPERATOR

Serenity Perimeter close to Salem and Twelfth. . . .

FIRST OPERATOR

Salem and Twelfth.

SECOND OPERATOR

Yes, Salem and Twelfth!

They reach up to "touch" the air a final time. Bells. Hums.

LANTRY'S VOICE

. . . wrong number . . . wrong number . . . wrong . . .

A final sizzle, a dance of light. A chord of music.

Blackout. Then lights up on LANTRY lying asleep. He stirs.

LANTRY

I wake at sunset with a dream of fire. I see myself pushed into the furnace, burned to ashes, then the ashes burnt to dust. God, can Dead men dream? (*Nods.*) And hate their dreaming. (*Listens.*) What? (*Raises his hand to touch out on the air.*) That building? It "*calls*" to me. I *must* . . . go there.

Exits into darkness.

The lights come up on: A library of the future.

A WOMAN sits amidst the "stacks," which are projected images of strangely shaped "books," of objects which, when picked up, begin to speak in tongues, recite themselves.

As A YOUNG MAN enters and whispers to her, she points to one side. He goes to pick up a "book" from its place where it is hung like a strange harp, to her left. He touches his hand to it. A soft voice murmurs.

THE VOICE

The square of the hypoteneuse . . . etc., etc.

A YOUNG WOMAN enters and is directed to the right, where she picks up a voice-book and brushes her hands across it as on a stringed instrument. It murmurs:

THE SECOND VOICE

The population of greater New York State, etc., etc.

ANOTHER MAN has entered, and is directed to a place

behind the woman, where his "book," touched, whispers:

THE THIRD VOICE

At the age of thirty-three, Hector Berlioz went to live in Rome, Italy. At that time he . . .

Music rises softly: Berlioz. Amidst all these voices, sounds, whispers, musics, LANTRY enters to the left, looks around, listens, ponders, turns.

LANTRY

Yes . . . yes, can it be? Odd, very strange, *but* a library. And . . . I'm lonely. I need friends. Special friends. People like . . . myself. Are there any in all the world? Or am I, oh Lord, dead and buried flesh, alone . . . alone? This might be the place to find out.

He steels himself, then turns, walks straight up to THE WOMAN at the desk amidst the murmurs and strange musics.

THE LIBRARIAN

Yes?

LANTRY

I would like to read . . . I mean . . . (*Stops; to himself.*) Careful.

He looks, listens, waits.

THE LIBRARIAN

Beg pardon?

LANTRY (*to himself*)

Careful. *Do* people read books, still? Or *watch* them like films? Or *play* them like toys?

He looks at the PEOPLE "playing their harp books," entranced. He turns back to the LIBRARIAN.

LANTRY
Ah . . . I would like, er . . . to *have* . . . Edgar Allan Poe?

THE LIBRARIAN (*puzzled*)
Sir?

LANTRY
Er . . . Poe. . . . Edgar Allan?

THE LIBRARIAN
Oh, that would be fiction, wouldn't it?

LANTRY
. . . yes. . . .

THE LIBRARIAN (*sniffs*)
Oh, we don't carry fiction, of course.

LANTRY (*stunned; aghast*)
No *fiction!*

THE LIBRARIAN (*finger to lip*)
Sh . . .

LANTRY (*lowering his voice*)
No fiction . . . ?

THE LIBRARIAN
But of course you *knew* that? Wait. I see. You're one of those odd ones from Mars! (*Laughs.*)

LANTRY
Just got back. Been there forever.

THE LIBRARIAN
But surely, even up there, they *told* you?

LANTRY
About . . . ?

THE LIBRARIAN (*with sacred awe*)
The Great Burning of Ten Years Back?

LANTRY
The Great Burning, of course.

THE LIBRARIAN (*proudly*)
We burned Mr. Poe.

LANTRY
Burned?

THE LIBRARIAN
And Mr. Dickens, and Mr. Hawthorne, and Mr. Melville. Burned, burned, burned. Oh, it was most lovely. They deserved to be given their rest.

LANTRY
Deserved?

THE LIBRARIAN
They weren't *real.* Never *were.* Dreamers, the lot. Nothing to do with reality, data, information.

LANTRY
And so you just . . . *killed* them?

THE LIBRARIAN
No, no, *burned* is more like it.

From the shadows, POE calls out softly.

POE
No, not killed . . . !

LANTRY hears, turns, wonders, sees nothing, turns back to the LIBRARIAN.

LANTRY
Burned . . . ?

THE LIBRARIAN
And Mr. Dickens.

DICKENS (*calls from the shadows*)
No!

THE LIBRARIAN
And Mr. Hawthorne!

HAWTHORNE (*as with the others*)
No, not a bit of it!

THE LIBRARIAN
And Mr. Melville!

MELVILLE (*with the others*)
Blast it, no!

THE LIBRARIAN
And Henry James, and Mr. Steinbeck, and
William Makepeace Thackeray and—

A ghostly CHORUS cries out: "No!" The four AUTHORS stand behind LANTRY, unlit, only shadows, half-seen. And behind them, projected perhaps, the GHOSTS of other authors, misting and reshaping, and reaching out. They sigh and murmur.

THE AUTHORS
Please . . . please, no . . . !

THE LIBRARIAN (*sweetly, smugly*)
Oh, it was most efficient-fine. They *should* have been put to rest centuries ago!

LANTRY
Should have?

THE AUTHORS
No . . . oh, no, no . . .

LANTRY hears, and turns, half-sees.

LANTRY
Yes, yes, there was a story once . . .

THE LIBRARIAN
A story?

LANTRY

Yes! A *fiction!* By a writer, can't recall . . . who wrote that all across Earth, the great names were burned. . . .

A sigh from the AUTHORS.

LANTRY

Most of their books, gone. . . .

THE AUTHORS (*whispering*)

. . . gone . . .

LANTRY

And so, these authors' ghosts, why they flew away to Mars . . . And survived there as written dreams, as wondrous fantasies, strange figments of old and dear imaginations. . . .

The AUTHORS stir and murmur, remembering.

LANTRY

Until one day, a rocket arrived from Earth with the Burners, the Censors, the Data-Collecting Destroyers who lived only by fact, and not by Dream. And brought with them the final books, the final lives of these final ghosts, and burned them on the sands of old dead Mars. . . .

Thunder and fire in the sky. LANTRY looks up, shades his eyes against the light, follows the fire and thunder down.

LANTRY

The rocket . . . the rocket!

The thunder fades. A ROCKET CAPTAIN stands forth out of darkness, an AIDE behind him carrying books. The captain himself has a list at which he glances.

LANTRY

The captain of the rocket! Oh, look! He smells of

menthol, iodine, and green soap. He is polished and manicured and oiled. His white teeth are dentrificed, his ears scoured to pinkness, as are his cheeks. His crisp hair is fresh cut and smells of alcohol. Even his breath is super sweet and new. There is no spot on him. And yet he comes to—

THE CAPTAIN (*cuts in; to himself*)
Kill.

THE AIDE
Sir?

THE CAPTAIN
Kill, quite frankly. Lay the final ghosts. You have the books, let's check the list. *Tales of Mystery and Imagination,* by Poe?

THE AIDE
Check. (*Checks list.*)

THE CAPTAIN
Dracula, by Bram Stoker.

THE AIDE
Check!

THE CAPTAIN
The Legend of Sleepy Hollow, by Washington Irving?

THE AIDE
Check!

THE CAPTAIN (*swiftly*)
The Turn of the Screw, by Henry James?

THE AIDE
Check!

THE CAPTAIN (*very crisply, swiftly*)
Frankenstein, by Mary Shelley? *Rappacini's*

Daughter, by Hawthorne. *Alice's Adventures in Wonderland*, by Carroll? *The Wizard of Oz*, by L. Frank Baum?

THE AIDE
Check, check, check, check!

THE AUTHORS' VOICES murmur and lament softly.

ALL (*whispering*)
Oh, no . . . oh, wait, wait! No . . . no. . . .

THE CAPTAIN
Lovecraft, Wells, Huxley, check, check, check, dump them all.

THE AIDE
They're dumped. (*Does so.*)

LANTRY
Oh, lost souls, look at *us* . . . look at *them*. Two rocket men. *Two* men against a legion, yet we fail. All along the desert shelves of Mars tonight, beyond us, look. Shakespeare's armies alone are multitudinous . . . there the three witches, there Oberon and Hamlet's father's ghost! There Richard and his murdered court and mighty armies of imagination and strange Time against, count them, two clean men who smell of soap and righteousness! Let us move!

ALL (*whispering*)
Move, yes, move!

THE CAPTAIN (*crisply*)
The flame!

THE AIDE
The flame. . . .

THE AIDE pantomimes a match to the books. Bright

flame-light bathes THE CAPTAIN only, with flickering fire-shadows.

THE CAPTAIN (*warms his hands in the light*)
So. So. So we dedicate ourselves to science and progress. So we destroy the dark past, and burn all superstition. So burn the monstrous names, the dreadful names of Cabell and Dunsany and Tolkien and Poe and Carroll and Lovecraft and Baum. So . . . so.

ALL
Oh! Oh . . . ! We die . . . we die . . . save us!

LANTRY
I will!

But he cannot move. Transfixed, he only "sees" the drama done.

THE CAPTAIN (*dryly*)
What, what was it the wicked witch said at the end of *The Wizard of Oz* when the bucket of water was tossed upon her?

THE AIDE (*tries to remember, and does*)
I . . . I'm *melting* . . . ?

THE CAPTAIN (*pleased, points to the books*)
I'm . . . melting.

ALL
Melting . . . melting. . . .

THE AUTHORS pull back into shadows, gone away, their voices fading.

LANTRY
No . . . please! Wait!

But they are gone. LANTRY has moved toward their area, but stops, for he is isolated, and the colors and lights of the library come up again and the PEOPLE "play" their books and soft voices sing data.

THE LIBRARIAN (*fades back in, reading her own list*)
Lovecraft, Baum, Burroughs! That's the full list. Oh, and Mr. Melville, of course, whoever *he* was.

LANTRY (*to himself*)
No! The man who birthed a whale, and now unknown! (*Turns and shouts at her.*) Do you know what you *are*?

THE LIBRARIAN (*startled*)
Sir!

LANTRY
A murderer! A murderer!

THE LIBRARIAN (*stands*)
Why, sir, I shall call the Peace Squad. You are in need of Peace. They will inject you.

LANTRY
Inject! Is there an injection, then, for my madness? (*Stops, gets hold of himself.*)

THE LIBRARIAN
You have been traveling, sir, a long way. The journey from Mars has tired you. I will *not* call the Squad.

LANTRY
Thanks. I'll be back. What day is this?

THE LIBRARIAN
Why, October 29, of course.

LANTRY (*snorts with the irony of it*)
Oh, good! I'll be back in two days, on Halloween.

THE LIBRARIAN
Halloween? You know there *isn't* any.

LANTRY (*a beat*)
No? They . . . burned *that*, too?

THE LIBRARIAN smiles and nods smugly. There is a great roar and crackling as of a huge and special fire, toward which LANTRY looks, stunned.

LANTRY
Murderers! Oh, yes . . . *murderers!*

He wanders off into darkness. THE LIBRARIAN, having jumped up at this last outburst of his, waits a beat, then sits and "dials."

THE LIBRARIAN
Q-112? Library here. . . . Peace Squad, please.

Blackout. Sirens. Motors. Voices. Then lights up again as LANTRY runs in, stops, looks back.

LANTRY
Oh, now, one *must* be careful. How strangely I am balanced in this world. Like some kind of dark gyroscope, whirling with never a murmur, a very silent man. (*Peers around.*) The street lights! How *dim* they are. And how *few!* It can't be—

YOUNG MAN (*passing by at this instant*)
Can't be what? (*Stares at Lantry.*)

LANTRY
Could you tell me, I mean . . .

YOUNG MAN
Tell you what?

LANTRY
Why there are so few street lights, and those so dim, and none in the middle of the blocks?

YOUNG MAN
Why?

LANTRY
You see, I'm a teacher. Merely testing your knowledge.

YOUNG MAN (*blankly*)
A teacher.

LANTRY
And it's *dark*.

YOUNG MAN
So?

LANTRY
Aren't you afraid?

YOUNG MAN
Of what?

LANTRY (*exasperated*)
The dark, of course, the dark!

YOUNG MAN (*calmly*)
Ho, ho!

LANTRY
Aren't *you*? Aren't *they*? Isn't *everyone!*

YOUNG MAN (*easily*)
Ho, ho, afraid, of the dark! Ha-hee! Wow, oh boy.

LANTRY
But street lights were invented *against* the dark, to *prevent* fear.

YOUNG MAN
Dumb. Of course that's not the reason. They were invented so you could see where you were walking or driving. But for no other reason. (*Shakes his head.*) *Real* dumb.

LANTRY
You mean to say you could walk down that street there, that unlit alley, and not be afraid?

YOUNG MAN (*snorts*)
Sure.

LANTRY
And go out in the hills and stay all night in the dark with no light?

YOUNG MAN
Sure.

LANTRY
And go in a haunted house and stay alone and not be frightened?

YOUNG MAN
A what?

LANTRY (*catches himself*)
Er . . . an empty house.

YOUNG MAN
Sure.

LANTRY
You lie! You lie! You lie! You must be afraid, I tell you, you *must!* You lie!

YOUNG MAN (*stops laughing; repeats as if by rote*)
Lie? I've never lied in my life. People don't lie. People don't lie. . . .

LANTRY
You lie!

YOUNG MAN
Only genetic inequitables lie. Only glandular inefficients lie. Only . . .

He peers at LANTRY.

YOUNG MAN
Boy, are you pale. Boy, are you white. I never seen anyone so pale, so white. Boy . . .

LANTRY (*moves threateningly*)
Aren't you afraid of me, for some reason?

YOUNG MAN (*calmly*)
No.

LANTRY (*puts one hand on the boy's shoulder*)
And . . . now?

YOUNG MAN
No.

LANTRY (*puts both hands on the young man's neck*)
And . . . now.

YOUNG MAN (*calmly*)
You may well be a genetic inequitable or most probably a glandular inefficient with the color of your skin, so . . . (*Shrugs.*)

A siren wails. LANTRY turns, backs off.

YOUNG MAN
Hey . . . wait. . . . I'll be darned. You're afraid. *You're* frightened. *You're* scared!

LANTRY
No! (*Runs; exits.*)

YOUNG MAN (*calls after*)
Don't be, oh, please, don't be. (*Thinks, laughs, calls.*) Mind the dark, there, mind the dark!

Blackout.

Out of darkness, we hear CHILDREN'S VOICES passing, laughing, crying.

THE CHILDREN

Trick or treat . . . ha ha . . . trick or treat . . . ! . . . thanks. . . . Trick . . . trick!

The voices fade as LANTRY enters, listening.

LANTRY

Oh, no! All *that* . . . gone? All Hallow's dead? No more trick or treat? No more the happy children and the chase for sweets? The endless journeys in the rare autumn dusks of towns all spearmint and Baby Ruth rewards?
Oh, *none* of that? Blind me! Of all the rank, gross, crawling, empty-mouthed stupidity. What fun is there in children, if you don't imagine things? Oh, unbrave new world that has such cowards in it. I am your enemy! And all men like me! Tell us you will burn us, we do not burn! Tell us we're forever dead, and then we move! Say there are no vampires in the world, and blood we seek! Tell me that I cannot walk, and walk I will. Put Murder by, and why, I'll resurrect it *whole!* I am, *en toto,* all impossible things come possible. You have birthed me with your damnable plain soda cracker and dumb tasteless stews boiled out of ignorances made new scientific faith. Sun is good, sun is all, say you? Well, so is night, so is dark, say I. Dark is horror, listen! Night is meant for contrast. You *must* be afraid, or, what use for life? There are no beginnings without an end, don't you see? Noon has no meaning without midnight, fools! Listen. Hear! (*Waits.*) No? Well, then, beware you stake-driving killers of Stoker and Poe, you burners of

Tolkien who assassinate Santa Claus of a Christmas Eve and crucify Christ forever. I will make night what it once was, the thing against which you futile, wise, smug, knowing men built and lit all your lanterned cities. I knock at your door. I wait. No Treats, no Fun in Scares and Frights? Well, then: immense and mighty Tricks from this Dark Child.

The lights dim swiftly as LANTRY exits and the GHOST CHILDREN go by a final time, crying softly "Trick or treat." Fading.

A light comes up on THE LIBRARIAN. THE SPACE-SHIP CAPTAIN moves briskly in to confront her.

BURKE (*the captain*)
Good evening.

THE LIBRARIAN
Oh, yes, it's Captain Burke, isn't it?

BURKE
Burke, that's right.

THE LIBRARIAN
Just back from Mars. It's been quite a night for your people.

BURKE
Mine?

THE LIBRARIAN
The other gentleman, a friend of yours, he said—

BURKE
Other? Gentleman?

THE LIBRARIAN
Very pale. Said he'd come back with you two days ago, from Mars.

BURKE
But no one came with me. I came alone.

THE LIBRARIAN
Oh, dear. Oh, dear. He was lying, then? People don't lie.

BURKE
People don't lie.

THE LIBRARIAN
People don't lie. (*Dials phone.*) Peace Squad, please.

The light fades as she repeats.

THE LIBRARIAN
Peace Squad, please.

THE YOUNG MAN, in his own light, speaks to a man in shadow.

YOUNG MAN
Walking along here he was, yes, walking. Walking. Asked me if I was afraid of the dark, can you imagine? Walking, he was. Me, I was walking because, well, my car broke down. But him, why, he seemed to be walking, walking, yes, walking, *walking*. . . .

The light fades, and pinspots come up alternately on the various people: THE LIBRARIAN, THE YOUNG MAN, BURKE, and SMITH, THE FIRST GRAVEDIGGER.

THE LIBRARIAN
Pale he was . . .

YOUNG MAN
Walking . . . walking . . .

SMITH (*with one hand to his throat*)
People don't kill. . . . People don't—

BURKE
People don't lie . . .

THE LIBRARIAN
People don't lie. . .

SMITH
People don't kill, people don't—

BURKE
People don't lie. . . .

ALL babble their lines, fading.

In a light to one side, Peace Squad Officer MC CLURE appears.

MC CLURE
Peace Squad Officer McClure.

LIBRARIAN (*brightly*)
Oh, yes!

MC CLURE
A man who *lied* was here?

LIBRARIAN
He said he came from Mars.

MC CLURE
A man whose crime was being pale—

LIBRARIAN
Oh, very pale!

MC CLURE (*to* BURKE)
No friend of yours?

BURKE
He *said* he was.

MC CLURE (*making notes on hand computer*)
An odd man, not from Mars, and pale, and full of lies—

SMITH (*the gravedigger*)
And killing, sir, killing, sir, *killing!*

MC CLURE
Astounding thought. (*Writes.*) But, killing, *too.*

A vast explosion. ALL turn. ALL look.

MC CLURE
And . . . going about . . . blowing up the Places of the Sun, the Hearthing Places, the Incinerators of Souls?

Explosions, explosions, explosions.

MC CLURE waits a beat, eyes the reddened sky, then exits.

Blackout.

LANTRY enters among the strewn bodies in a make-shift morgue. We see the images of the laid-out dead, sheet-covered, on the scrims behind him, and on the floors about him.

LANTRY
What's this? A temporary morgue? Yes, yes. With all the Incinerators blown up by me, nowhere for all the bodies, except here, a high school gymnasium. Well . . .

LANTRY moves among the shadows and the forms.

LANTRY
Yes. (*A beat.*) Yes! (*Gestures all about, fondly, as to his children.*) Only a moment, and you'll be good as new. Friends? (*Nods.*) Friends. Let me see some of you. . . .

Moves among them, reading names on tags or blouses.

LANTRY
Griswold, Hart, Remington, good. You'll rise and

walk with me and make more dead. (*Bends, reads.*) Carruthers. An architect! Yes! Now, listen, Carruthers, when you awake and rise, we will rebuild the House of Usher! And build us anthropoids to prowl its midnight halls; sweet robot apes that, ticking madly, will find and keep the best learned sociologists of this clean time and stuff them up the chimneys! Even as that orang-utan run wild in the Rue Morgue did fix a body up a flue! Red Deaths we will build and wind and wander free to spread a robot plague and teach men what's not been taught in years: to dread the dark, to fear a spider hand, to flee from daggers and from guns.... So at the end of all our building, with the grand gorillas, maddened black cats, stalking Plagues, we'll run the pack of brilliant teachers, learners, doers, to the android catacombs and there wall up their cries with bricks and casks of, oh, now, yes! Amontillado! And then stand back, and press the switch which breaks the dungeons down, lets water in! So Phantom of the Opera, Wax Works, murderers, dumb robot apes, and sociologists, psychologists, biting, yapping, snapping at their own tails, sink down, as Usher Two falls to rocks, and dust and oblivions lost to sight.

We hear the falling of the house into the lake, far off.

LANTRY (*a beat*)
Will you build this with me? (*Nods, satisfied.*) I think you will. As for the rest? Soon enough, you'll know.... Now!

MC CLURE enters unseen and watches as LANTRY busies himself with chalk taken from his pocket.

LANTRY

Pentagrams, symbols, thus, and so. Symbols, pentagrams here, now there. And *there!*

He has marked the sheets of the dead. Now he draws a great circle on the floor to enclose himself and many of the forms.

LANTRY

Are we prepared? We *are!* So now, arise!
Arise, ye dead. Arise, my brothers, sisters, stir, then go with me! Live! Live! By all that is unholy, or, why not? holy! live!

No motion. Nothing stirs.

LANTRY

You've been marked! I say the words! I do command! Rise up! Rise! (*Stunned now, and uncomprehending.*) No? But the mark is so—! (*Scribbles more symbols on the floor.*) And the words are thus: Be alive!

Nothing stirs. All is silence.

LANTRY

But you must! Why not! Why won't you rise to *be* with me? In all the years, the centuries, you *always* have! These signs, these words have done it! But *not* to *you?*

The sound of a jet flies over. He watches the sound move. A siren wails, a long way off.

Slowly LANTRY's shoulders sag, his face grows bleak.

LANTRY

Oh, plague take me for a fool. Fool. (A *beat.*)
O ancient fool. This is the year . . .

MC CLURE (*quietly*)
2274.

MC CLURE has been standing to one side for a long while now, waiting, smoking.

LANTRY (*startled*)
What?

MC CLURE (*quietly*)
2274.

LANTRY
Oh, yes, the year.

MC CLURE
Very late in time. Very late for you.

LANTRY
How long have you been standing there?

MC CLURE
Awhile.

LANTRY
You saw it all?

MC CLURE nods, blows smoke slowly.

LANTRY
These won't *move!*

MC CLURE
Why should they? They're dead.

LANTRY
Once people shuddered when they heard the wind about the house, once people raised crucifixes and wolfbane, and believed in walking dead and bats and loping wolves. And as long as they believed, why, then, so long did the dead, the bats, the loping wolves exist. Mind made them flesh. But these . . . *these?*

He nods to the quiet forms, which MC CLURE quietly regards.

MC CLURE

They don't *believe.* They never in all their *lives* believed. They had never read or talked or known of the walking dead, never traded superstitions, never shuddered in the night or doubted darkness. These were raised in menthol and cleansed with soap and salt and rinsed in medicines and spun dry-clean. They know no ghosts, they have no ghosts. Bones are simply bones to such as these. That being true . . .

LANTRY

. . . they cannot rise, or walk away.

MC CLURE

No chalk can sign or symbol make them breathe. No lengthy diatribe can slap them, wind them up and run them to destruction. They are dead and *know* they are dead, and, *knowing,* stay cold forever. Which means—these are *not* your friends.

LANTRY

I hoped that they *might* be. . . .

A beat. MC CLURE considers his hand computer.

MC CLURE

You *are,* then, William Lantry?

LANTRY

I *was.*

MC CLURE

Born 1973, died 2003?

LANTRY

The same.

MC CLURE
We've been looking for you.

LANTRY
The Peace Squad?

MC CLURE
No, no, oh, no. The Geriatrics Society, The Specialists in Suspended Animation, the Scientists who study Cryonics! You are special! You are amazing! And they all want to meet you!

LANTRY
After what I've done?

MC CLURE
You've done nothing but sleep in suspended animation for two hundred years!

LANTRY (*stunned*)
No!

MC CLURE
Yes! Oh, we've known suspended animation with small animals, toads, frogs, insects, yes, but a mature man, hardly.

LANTRY (*stunned*)
But you saw me mark the bodies?

MC CLURE
I did.

LANTRY
I tried to raise the dead.

MC CLURE
You did.

LANTRY
I blew up the Incinerators, killed people . . .

MC CLURE

My dear Lantry, you acted in delusion! You're not a dead man, you're no kin to Dracula or Poe. Oh, I know the names. I have a few books put by in secret. You're a common ordinary soul who has survived and slept out the years, and now, awake, was struck with a silly idea that somehow he represented the last of the dead!

LANTRY

But I killed people! Now you must kill me!

MC CLURE

What? Destroy a singular medical miracle like you, the first man in history to survive underground for over two hundred years? You'll be in all the media! Films! Television!

LANTRY (*touches himself*)

No, no! Even now, I don't breathe! My heart doesn't beat, my blood move, no, listen, *feel!*

MC CLURE

Subliminal nonsense. (*Seizes Lantry's wrist.*) It's all there. You pretend it's not.

LANTRY (*feels his own heart and pulse*)

Not? Not? But . . . I was so sure . . . ?

MC CLURE

Just enjoy being a resurrected human being! Come along, come on!

LANTRY (*almost pitifully*)

Then . . . I'm not a dangerous man . . . at *all?*

MC CLURE

Dangerous? Naturally you deluded yourself, didn't know where to go, whom to turn to. Finding yourself in a graveyard that way,

what else but you confused yourself. You
made quite a trail. I knew you'd be here, tonight,
in this morgue. Call it a hunch, a feeling . . .

LANTRY
But . . . but . . . it's very strange. *Why haven't I been hungry yet?*

MC CLURE
Why, you're excited. Hunger will come in time.
Come along.

LANTRY
Must I meet all your scientists, tonight?

MC CLURE
No, of course not. Now I'm the one who plays the
excited fool. Forgive. You'll come to my home, to
rest, to sleep . . .

LANTRY
I've slept two hundred years.

MC CLURE
Forgive. Well, then, it's food and drink and talk.
You must *tell* me of the *Past!*

LANTRY
No. You must tell *me* of the *Future!*

Both laugh, and there is an embarrassed silence.

LANTRY turns away suddenly, to himself.

LANTRY (*to himself*)
It's a trap! A trap!

MC CLURE (*touches his elbows*)
What's wrong?

LANTRY (*ducks his head, chafes his elbows: to himself*)

A trap. He lies. He must lie. I *am* the dark thing that I *am!* Not the bright angel of resurrection that *he* says. (*Turns to look at McClure numbly.*) I think that I should kill you and escape.

MC CLURE
What, still wallowing in graveyard worms and dust?

MC CLURE circles him slowly as he talks.

MC CLURE
All right, let's argue it from your angle.
Suppose I *am* lying. Suppose you *are* dead, and
I know you for dead. Suppose I did come up to
you five minutes ago thinking you were
some sort of glandular deficient, some
inequitable citizen, eh? But then, watching
you, saw you hold your breath, kidding
yourself you were dead. Slowed your pulse,
fooling yourself you were bad flesh, old corpse.
Such delusions *are* known in history. And
then, let us imagine, in watching you, I truly
never saw you take one breath, and now
close up, in the still night air, I sense,
I know, your dead heart does not beat, not
beat!

LANTRY
And? *Then? THEN?*

LANTRY reaches out and takes MC CLURE by the neck. McClure remains calm.

MC CLURE
Well, then, *what* if you kill me?

LANTRY
It would satisfy my lust!

MC CLURE
For what? Simply to kill the nice efficient, un-hung-up people of a future time whose only crime is they are happy at midnight, and fear not closet shadows? And have let the Halloween pumpkin rot forever neglected?

LANTRY
Yes, that *is* a crime!

LANTRY tightens his hold on MC CLURE's neck, but McClure refuses to panic, waits. Lantry relaxes his grip somewhat.

MC CLURE
Let's take it one step further. You seek to kill to make friends.

LANTRY
Yes, friends!

MC CLURE (*points to the bodies nearby*)
And yet you've seen, you have no friends. These dead are dead forever.

LANTRY
I will kill more!

MC CLURE
And *they* will be dead forever.

LANTRY
You! *You*, I'll kill!

MC CLURE
And *I* shall be dead forever. I will not rise up to help you. I will not come to the aid of your single and singular party.

LANTRY
I will kill everyone on Earth!

MC CLURE
To what avail or cause? Why, then you would be finally and completely *alone*.

Eyes shut, LANTRY shrivels at these words.

MC CLURE (*continues*)
Kill one, kill all, kill millions, kill me, and you're no better off than you are this instant standing here wanting to throttle a man who throttles back with simple logics and inescapable fact. There is no winning, Lantry. You are lost now and you might be lost tomorrow. These dead have no dark corners in them. They have no superstition. I have none. You are friendless and unloved.

LANTRY (*weakly*)
I *can't* give up.

MC CLURE (*simply*)
Give up.

LANTRY opens his hands. MC CLURE does not move. He nods a final time, this motion causing the hands to fall away.

LANTRY stands, almost catatonic.

MC CLURE (*with sympathy*)
Don't you see that hate is what brought you into the world? But now that you know yourself truly alone, loneliness is the thing that will kill you?

LANTRY
Loneliness . . . ?

MC CLURE
It kills everyone, finally, when they truly know themselves separate. One day it will even kill me.

LANTRY
Will it?

MC CLURE (*gently*)
You know it will.

LANTRY has been examining his hands, touching his own body, trying to reconvince himself during all the above. Now he cries out and raises his fists, turning toward MC CLURE as if to move upon and strike him.

LANTRY
No! No! Shut up! Shut up!

At which point TWO MEN enter and stop, curious, somewhat amazed.

FIRST OFFICER
What's going on? A new game?

MC CLURE
Yes, a new game! Catch him and you win!

LANTRY's fury explodes toward the men. MC CLURE steps back as Lantry traps himself by plunging directly into their arms. They hold his arms behind his back as he struggles.

SECOND OFFICER
We win.

LANTRY
Fools! Fools! Let me go!

MC CLURE
Hold him tight!

FIRST OFFICER
A rough game, what? What do we do now?

MC CLURE (*a beat*)
To the Hearthing Place.

FIRST OFFICER
The Place of the Sun?

LANTRY (*shocked; almost to himself*)
. . . the Incinerator!

They begin to move. LANTRY holds back, but then gives up and moves along as MC CLURE speaks.

MC CLURE
Oh, it's been hard, hard to accept you. A man like me, a logical man, from my own age and time. But, shall I tell you something?

LANTRY
What? What!

They stop for a beat. MC CLURE looks into LANTRY'S face.

MC CLURE
You almost . . . *frighten* me.

LANTRY is shocked and almost pleased by this.

LANTRY
You . . . me . . . ? *You* . . . ?

MC CLURE (*nods*)
Frightened.

He nods a second time to the men. They move in a great circle through darkness now.

LANTRY
Well, then, that means, oh Lord, that means . . . I *am* Poe. I am all that is left of Edgar Allan Poe, and I am all that is left of Ambrose Bierce and Lovecraft . . .

A light appears behind them: the glow of the Furnace, the Incinerator, the Place of the Sun. They move in a great circle through darkness around the stage.

LANTRY
. . . I am Osiris and Bal and Set. I am the

Necronomican, the Book of the Dead. I am the House of Usher, I am the Red Death, I am a coffin, a shroud, a lightning bolt reflected in an old house window. I am an autumn-empty tree, I am a yellowed book page turned by a claw-hand . . . I am an organ played in an attic at midnight. I am a mask, a skull mask behind an oak tree on the last day of October. I am . . .

They have stopped now, and we see behind them the orange-yellow glow, the open maw of the Incinerator, the Place of the Sun. The TWO MEN dance aside for a moment, leaving LANTRY to sway, fumbling at his own thoughts, supported for a moment by MC CLURE. McClure pantomimes to the two men to go fetch something.

LANTRY
. . . I am a poison apple bobbling in a water tub for children's teeth to snap . . . I am a black candle lit before an inverted cross. I am a sugar skull with my name on it to be eaten . . .

The TWO MEN are back with vast swatches of linen wrapping, which, as LANTRY watches, stunned, they begin to wrap around his ankles and then up along his legs as Lantry continues speaking, almost chanting, hypnotizing himself with his own recital.

LANTRY
. . . I am a coffin lid, a sheet with eyes, I am the Legend of Sleepy Hollow and I am the Monkey's Paw and the Phantom Rickshaw. . . . I am the Pit and I am the Pendulum . . .

MC CLURE (*gently, urging him on*)
. . . yes . . .

LANTRY
I am the Cat and the Canary, the Gorilla, the Bat.
I am Hamlet's father's dead and buried ghost. . . .

The MEN move up, up, wrapping, wrapping him into a mummy. Now they are at his hips, circling the linen bandages around and around, passing it from hand to hand, efficient at their shroudwork.

LANTRY
All of these things am I . . . while I lived, they lived . . . while I moved and hated and existed, they still existed. I am all that remembers them, and will *not* remember them after tonight. To-night, all of us, Poe and Red Death and Roderick Usher, we *burn!* Like straw scarecrows at Guy Fawkes you will make a heap of all our panics and terrors and touch a match and burn!

The MEN move steadily, calmly. They have bound his arms now around-about-around-about with the white linen mummy bandages, not even listening to him rave and chant. Only MC CLURE listens, nods, and quietly reaffirms it all.

MC CLURE
Yes . . . yes . . .

LANTRY
And oh what a wailing we will put up. The world will be clean of us, but in our going we shall say, oh, what is the world like, clean of Fear? Where is the dark imagination from the dark time, the thrill, the anticipation, the suspense of old October, gone, never more to be, smashed and burned by the rocket people, the Incinerator people, destroyed and obliterated, to be replaced by doors that open and close with no shrieks or cries

and lights that go on and off without fear. Oh, by the dark gods, if only you *knew* how once we lived, what Halloween *was* to us! how we gloried in the dark morbidities! The time is *here*, those ghosts are *here*, in my head, my thoughts, my dreams! I *drink* to them! The Amontillado!

MC CLURE
Yes, the Amontillado. . . .

They have finished with LANTRY's body now and wrap steadily up about his face, his chin, and one swathe over his nose, and another over his brow, leaving his eyes wildly seeing, and his mouth wildly moving.

LANTRY
Someone's at the door. Quick, oh quickly!
The Monkey's Paw! Make the wish, the wish!

MC CLURE (*gently*)
The wish, yes, the wish.

The fire grows bright behind them. A great heart sounds, *beats!*

LANTRY
I am the Maelstrom, the Black Cat, I am the Tell-tale Heart, I am the Raven Nevermore, Nevermore.

The MEN are done. They have put a last swathe across his eyes. But his mouth can be seen as he finishes.

LANTRY
I am Dracula. I am the Phantom of the Opera.

MC CLURE
Yes.

MC CLURE nods to the MEN, who carry LANTRY backward toward the Fire. Lantry senses this, twists his head left and right, blindly.

LANTRY

I am in . . . the Catacomb?

MC CLURE

The catacomb.

MC CLURE nods to the TWO OFFICERS. The men grasp and begin to hoist LANTRY.

LANTRY

I am being chained to a wall, but there is no bottle of Amontillado!

MC CLURE

None.

LANTRY

Now someone is mortaring up the cell, closing me in!

MC CLURE

They are.

LANTRY

I'm trapped. A very good joke indeed. Let us be gone!

MC CLURE

Yes, gone.

MC CLURE nods a final time to the MEN who hold the "mummy" suspended above the chute. The fire is bright. The great telltale heart pounds loud, louder, loudest.

LANTRY

For the love of God, Montresor!

They tilt him swiftly over and down the chute, away, gone. The fire roars. The Telltale Heart stops pounding.

Turned away, eyes shut, unable to watch, MC CLURE waits for the color of the fire to die behind him, two or three beats. Then he speaks.

MC CLURE (*with compassion*)
Oh, yes. For the love of God.

Lights dim swiftly. Blackout. Curtain.

Kaleidoscope

At curtain rise: darkness.
Static, electronic sounds, radio impulses.

Then, a radio impulse, twice, three times.

HOUSTON RADIO VOICE
Signal RD Houston calling. Space Flight Apollo 99 respond.

HOLLIS (*on radio*)
Apollo 99. Hollis here.

HOUSTON RADIO
Loud and clear. Medical checkout. Soma tapes running. By the numbers.

HOLLIS appears in silhouette, his face dimly illuminated. We can see that he stands amidst his CREW, all of them closely packed in a small crowd. Ideally these men should be located in the orchestra pit with their heads and shoulders above the sight lines, and the entire stage area free for later use. As each man speaks, his own individual illumination comes on until the entire crew is seen compacted into what must be the interior of a space ship. As the men respond, they pantomime with their hands as if moving the controls or the radio equipment of such a ship.

HOLLIS (*his spot comes on*)
Hollis. Physical report to Houston medico/soma tapes. A-1.

STONE (*appears*)
Stone here. A-1.

STIMSON (*appears*)
Stimson. A-1.

APPLEGATE (*appears*)
Good old Applegate here. In fine fettle.

HOLLIS (*curtly*)
Applegate!

APPLEGATE (*ducks his head*)
Hell. A-1.

LESPERE (*appears*)
Lespere. Okay.

BARKLEY (*appears*)
Barkley. Super A-1.

WOODE
Woode reporting. Fine, thanks.

APPLEGATE
All present and accounted f—

He stops, for HOLLIS has given him a look.

HOLLIS
All present and well. Nine days and three million, four hundred thousand miles out from Earth.

HOUSTON RADIO
Check. Psycho-balance tapes operative. Scramble thoughts. Word associate.

APPLEGATE
Stupid.

HOUSTON RADIO
Repeat, please.

APPLEGATE
Not only *how* we feel but *what* we feel, to a computerized psychoanalyst three million miles away! Stupid!

HOLLIS (*cuts in*)
Applegate!

APPLEGATE
Now hear this: A for Applegate. H for Horse. S for Snowstorm. R.P. for Rabbit Pellets. Enough word association?

HOUSTON VOICE
Terminate, Applegate.

APPLEGATE
Terminate Applegate? (*Snorts.*) That's *poetry!*

HOLLIS (*cool and quiet*)
Terminate. (*A beat.*) Hollis here.

HOUSTON RADIO
Scramble-associate, Hollis.

HOLLIS (*a beat; he swallows; then:*)
Sometimes I wonder why I am captain of a rocket bound into deep space.

The MEN look at him, waiting.

HOLLIS
And then I remember that not all of my crew members are named Applegate.

APPLEGATE (*mock miffed*)
Hey . . . !

The CREW laughs.

HOUSTON RADIO
End of Hollis scramble?

HOLLIS
End.

STIMSON
Stimson here.

HOUSTON RADIO
Scramble-associate, Stimson.

STIMSON
It took me two days to get to the top of Saint Peter's in Rome. Three days to nerve myself to make it to the top of the Eiffel Tower. Sometimes I wonder what I'm doing, three million miles high in space.

The MEN murmur.

STIMSON (*shuts eyes*)
End scramble.

WOODE
Woode here. I . . . I *never* made it to the top of the Eiffel Tower. I was . . . afraid.

HOUSTON VOICE (*mocking*)
Now you tell us, Woode.

The MEN laugh, gently, understandingly.

WOODE (*nods, shrugs*)
Now I tell you.

LESPERE
Lespere scrambling. Hot dogs. Apple pie. Mom.

APPLEGATE
Hey, what kind of word association is that?

LESPERE
Midnight. Open the icebox door. Reach in. Three-layer banana cake. Glass of milk. Yes, *sir!*

APPLEGATE
He's kidding.

LESPERE
Sand-lot baseball.

APPLEGATE
He's nuts!

LESPERE
Good cigars. Grandpa and Dad talking late at night on the front porch rocking chairs.

APPLEGATE
I may throw up!

LESPERE
Over and out scramble.

STONE
Stone in. I—

Bells, sirens, static, radio impulses.

HOLLIS
Stone, Woode, Lespere?

STONE
Meteor dead on! Impact! Impact! Prepare for collision!

The MEN hold to each other, in one fierce wild crowd for an instant, then reach out their hands as if to hold off collision, and work, in pantomime, their various machines and computers. Bells ring. Rapid impulses run wild!

HOLLIS
Crew to stations. Oxygen helmets! Helmets on! Helmets on!

We see them, in pantomime, clap on their helmets and oxygen equipment. Sirens blare.

HOLLIS
On stations, all?

LESPERE
On! We . . . Oh, my God! Impact! Im—

Instant darkness. The MEN vanish.

A fearful explosion. Static and radioactive sounds. Voices cry and shout. ALL fade in and out.

VOICES (*on radio, rising, fading*)
. . . Oh, God, falling, falling . . .
ship . . . where's the rocket? Explosion! Gone!
Where, where? . . . Captain? . . . Stone? The men,
the men, where're the men? . . . Captain? . . . Gone,
gone . . . Oh, falling, falling!

One face, that of CAPTAIN HOLLIS, appears, pinspotted, higher now, up on stage left in a kaleidoscope of shifting lights, shadows, stars. He looks all about, terrified, then gradually regains his wits and his speech. Slowly, he pieces it together.

HOLLIS
Oh, the concussion! Like a giant knife had cut it,
the rocket just . . . split wide! The men, oh . . .
thrown out in space. Like, like a dozen wriggling
silverfish. Scattered in a dark sea. And the rocket,
in a million pieces, there it goes, a meteor-swarm
seeking a lost sun . . . gone . . . oh, gone.

VOICES (*over radio*)
Barkley, Barkley, where are you? . . . Woode,
Woode . . . ? Captain?

HOLLIS
Voices . . . calling like lost children in a long
night. . . .

VOICES
Captain . . . Barkley . . . where, where? Woode?

STONE'S VOICE
Captain Hollis, Captain . . . ? This is Stone!

HOLLIS (*quickens*)
Stone, Hollis here. Where are you? (*Stops.*)
Stupid, stupid question! Where?

STONE (*his face appears floating in the dark off to one side*)
God knows, *I* don't! Which way is up? I only
know I'm falling, falling . . .

HOLLIS
Yes, we fall. Like pebbles down a well. We're not
men anymore, not captain, crew . . . only voices
. . . voices without bodies . . .

STONE
We're going away from each other . . . !

HOLLIS
Oh, yes, that's for sure. At one hundred thousand
miles an hour! Here's your hat, what's your hurry?
We *do* move.

STONE
What happened?

HOLLIS
A meteor strike. The rocket blew up. Rockets *do*
blow up.

STONE (*numbly*)
They do, oh, they do. Is . . . is there any way
for us to get back to one another, get together?

HOLLIS

Not unless you strapped on your force-fly unit just before the blowup?

STONE

No. You?

HOLLIS

There wasn't time. So here we are, seven men dropped in space, with no way to maneuver, turn, fly. All we can do is . . .

STONE

. . . fall . . .

STIMSON'S VOICE (*on radio*)

. . . fall . . . fall . . . Oh, it's a long way . . . long way . . . a long, long, long way down . . .

STONE

Who's that?

HOLLIS

Stimson, I think. (*Calls.*) Stimson!

Now STIMSON's pinpoint light fades up. We see him floating above and beyond the other two.

STIMSON

. . . long way down . . . long way . . . I'm going to die. I can't *believe* that. I—

HOLLIS

Stimson! Let's get organized here!

Now APPLEGATE's face light flashes on as he hoots with laughter. He floats, moves, now up, now down, only his face visible.

APPLEGATE

Organized? Organized! Listen to the man! Organized!

HOLLIS
Applegate, is that you?

APPLEGATE
Applegate, scared gutless but reporting. Boy, you're funny, Captain.

HOLLIS
What do you *want* me to do, let us all go to Hell?

APPLEGATE
You're not in *charge* anymore, Captain. We go where we *go*.

HOLLIS
Roll call, anyway, damn it!

APPLEGATE
Roll call! (*Hoots again.*)

HOLLIS
So help me, we're going to die decently. By the names, check in! Stone?

STONE (*nods*)
Stone here.

HOLLIS
Lespere?

LESPERE (*whose light comes on now*)
Lespere here.

HOLLIS
Barkley?

BARKLEY (*his light comes on*)
Still alive. Barkley.

HOLLIS
Woode?

Silence. We see WOODE's face, alone, illuminated, above

the men, floating. But his eyes are tight shut, his teeth gritted. He is shut away in himself, in panic.

APPLEGATE
Make him answer, Captain.

HOLLIS
Woode?

Static and far electronic angel voices in space. WOODE drifts off, as his light slowly fades.

APPLEGATE
Like I said, Captain, you're not in charge.

HOLLIS (*cuts across*)
Stimson?

STIMSON (*numbly*)
Stimson, who's *he?* Oh, yes . . . *he's* . . . falling . . .

APPLEGATE, hearing this, quiets, is moved by the sound of that far voice.

APPLEGATE
I—

STIMSON (*numbly*)
Falling, that's what *he* is, falling.

APPLEGATE (*quietly*)
Take it easy, we're all in the same fix.

STIMSON (*dreaming*)
I don't want to be here, I want to be somewhere else.

APPLEGATE (*dryly*)
You can say that again.

HOLLIS
All right, Applegate.

APPLEGATE (*flaring again*)
All right, *what?*

HOLLIS
We haven't much time.

APPLEGATE
Time, gah! We got all the Time in the world, and all of Space in the Universe. That's all we *do* have, Space and Time!

HOLLIS (*quietly, as calm as possible*)
We're moving away from each other. We'll soon lose radio contact.

APPLEGATE
Can't happen soon enough for me. I won't have to hear any of your stupid voices.

HOLLIS
Why do you insist on being bitter?

APPLEGATE
Look around you, Captain. Where are you? Nowhere. Where'm I? Beyond nowhere. Where's everyone else? Falling to die. The rocket spun when it was hit. We were thrown off by centrifugal force, each man in a different direction. Some of us will hit the sun. Some of us will head out through the Universe and travel forever. Bitter? How can you *say* that?

STONE
Captain?

HOLLIS
Stone?

STONE
Might we get back together somehow? I mean—

APPLEGATE
For *what*, what, *what!?*

HOLLIS
To die in company, now that you ask.

APPLEGATE
You *do* that, then. I'll die alone, thanks, at one hundred thousand miles per hour.

STONE
If each of us released a certain amount of oxygen, we could maneuver—

APPLEGATE
Keep talking. Your hot air would fill a dozen balloons and save us all.

STIMSON (*numbly*)
Please, someone help me, I don't want to be here. I don't want to be here.

HOLLIS
Stimson.

APPLEGATE
That's it, Captain, order him to shut up. (*Calls.*) Hey, Stimson, listen to the captain.

HOLLIS (*uneasily*)
Stimson! We can't *talk* if you interrupt. I mean—

STIMSON (*like a child*)
Help, oh, someone help, so far down, a long way down, falling, falling, oh, such a long way down. . . .

HOLLIS
Stimson . . .

APPLEGATE (*stares up, gasps*)
Hold on! Oh, *now* . . . you're not going to believe this!

STIMSON
Help, oh, please, help, I'm afraid!

HOLLIS
Applegate?

APPLEGATE
Captain, he's *here!*

HOLLIS
What?

APPLEGATE
Stimson! He's floating nearby. I can *see* him! We're getting closer!

STIMSON
Oh, such a long way down, falling, falling, a long, long way. Help. Help.

APPLEGATE
Yes, I'll help you, Stimson.

HOLLIS (*apprehensive, guessing at Applegate's motive*)
Applegate?

STIMSON
I don't *like* being here.

APPLEGATE (*softly*)
You *won't* be much longer.

STIMSON
I want to be somewhere else.

APPLEGATE (*patiently, quietly*)
You will, you will.

HOLLIS
Applegate!

APPLEGATE
Closer, oh, very close, Captain. He's floating almost in reach . . . almost . . .

STIMSON
Oh, I'm afraid, someone help. . . .

APPLEGATE (*gently*)
Help, yes.

STIMSON
Someone . . . someone . . .

APPLEGATE
Me. . . .

HOLLIS
Applegate!

STIMSON
Someone, oh, please, someone . . . ?

APPLEGATE
Me!

STIMSON (*cries out*)
Some—!

In mid-cry, STIMSON's voice cracks to a complete shut-off. His light vanishes.

There is a beat, and then HOLLIS whispers in dread.

HOLLIS
Applegate . . . ?

APPLEGATE (*eyes shut*)
He's gone, Captain.

HOLLIS
Gone . . . ?

APPLEGATE
I smashed his helmet.

HOLLIS
You—?

APPLEGATE (*simply*)
He wanted to be saved. (*Opens eyes.*) I saved him.

All the MEN exhale in a moment of quiet.

HOLLIS (*quietly*)
Yes.

APPLEGATE (*a beat*)
Approved?

HOLLIS (*a beat*)
Approved.

Radio static swarms. There is a long moment when the MEN move with their own thoughts, turning.

APPLEGATE
Now we can talk more clearly, Captain. Now, if you want, we can get "organized."

HOLLIS
Applegate?

APPLEGATE
Sir?

HOLLIS
May you *burn* forever!

APPLEGATE
Why, sir, I'm on my way to burning now. From the way I fall, I figure in about half a year, I'll strike the Sun. How about you others, Stone, Lespere, Barkley? Where *heading*, for how *long*?

STONE
I . . . I think I'm going to hit the Moon.

BARKLEY
I'm . . . I think . . . I'm heading for Mars. Can't really say, but, well, Mars.

LESPERE
Mars and Beyond, Jupiter, Saturn, maybe visit Pluto, or go on into the Universe and travel forever, that's me—far-traveling. Doesn't that have a sound to it? Far-traveling.

APPLEGATE
Captain?

Silence.

APPLEGATE
Captain?

HOLLIS
I . . . I seem to be heading back toward Earth. When I hit its atmosphere . . . ?

APPLEGATE
You'll burn, long before me.

HOLLIS (*swallows hard, eyes shut*)
I'll burn. (*A beat.*) Silence!

APPLEGATE
Order me some more. This is a mutiny of one. In just the few minutes since the rocket exploded, you and I have moved ten thousand miles away from each other. But we were *always* far apart! Come get me, sir. Shall I tell you some more that will make you want to come get me?

HOLLIS
Do your worst.

APPLEGATE
And the worst is this. Years ago, when we were at the Academy, your fiancée, that lovely girl, remember . . .

HOLLIS
No, it never *was*.

APPLEGATE
It was . . .

HOLLIS
No, Earth's *gone* now, I can't *see* it.

APPLEGATE
It's there.

HOLLIS (*turns head away*)
No, it's like it never was. Green fields, towns, rivers, lakes, gone, all gone . . . so far away and only night now and stars, too many stars. . . .

APPLEGATE
No, there *was* this girl, and she left you, you want to know why, shall I *tell* you why?

HOLLIS
No, she never lived!

APPLEGATE
She lived.

HOLLIS
There is no Earth, no life, nothing.

APPLEGATE
There was life and earth and something. And I took it all away.

HOLLIS
You took nothing, nothing!

STONE (*cuts in*)
Ah, no! No more, no more of this!

HOLLIS (*in an agony of remorse*)
No more!

APPLEGATE (*shamed by their reaction at last*)
No . . . more.

LESPERE (*a beat*)
I'm amazed.

APPLEGATE
Eh?

LESPERE
I'm astounded.

APPLEGATE
What?

LESPERE
We're all going to be dead in a few hours, and you . . . go on like this? Can't you leave us to remember . . . ?

APPLEGATE
What?

LESPERE
Good things. Good, yes! The *best!*

APPLEGATE
What was ever best, what good?

LESPERE
My life, maybe not yours, but mine!

APPLEGATE
How was it better?

LESPERE
Let me make the list! A wife on Earth. Good friends on the Moon! My children on Mars!

APPLEGATE
And?

LESPERE
A wife on Earth, friends on the Moon, my sons and daughters safe on Mars!

APPLEGATE
What else?

LESPERE (*doggedly does the rote*)
My wife, my friends, my—

APPLEGATE
That's no *list!*

LESPERE
Better than a list, it's a *life!*

STONE (*calmly, almost to himself*)
I'm going to kill all of you in ten minutes.

APPLEGATE (*startled*)
Kill *us?*

STONE
Just by opening my helmet. I'll freeze solid in a millionth of a second . . . and you'll all disappear forever! Strange. The quickest death in the history of mankind . . . and invented not on Earth but a million miles out in space . . . I'll freeze and be frozen forever . . . think, think of it . . . if I should not hit the Moon but circle it for a million years, and a rocket came by and found me, I wouldn't have changed. Out in space, nothing ever changes. A billion

years from tonight I'll be circling and young, still only this age, and my body frozen, not spoiled or grown old . . . a billion years from tonight . . . think . . . *think!*

APPLEGATE

I'm thinking: kill yourself now and cut the cackle.

LESPERE

I'm thinking that we should all say what we want to say in these last few minutes. I want to run my films, play my memories, say *there* was a good day, *there* a bad, there a good friend . . . Gah! You know what I mean.

APPLEGATE

No, I don't, because it never happened, like the captain says, once a thing is over it's like it never existed. *We* only exist now, a mob of voices floating half into nowhere and out of nothing.

LESPERE

No, I *count*, because I remember, I *do* remember!

APPLEGATE

Do you? (*Curiously.*) Do you really? Well. Maybe that's why I've gotten mean in my middle years. All my life, I kept waiting for something to happen. I mean *something*. But . . . it never did.

LESPERE

Man, man, you've been in space, you've circled the Sun, landed on Mars! What *more* do you want?

APPLEGATE

I don't know, isn't that funny? I just don't . . . Wait! (*Gasps; stares down in shock.*) Well, now, hear this. I . . . have no left hand.

LESPERE
What?

HOLLIS
Applegate!

APPLEGATE (*still in shock, but operative*)
No kidding. Strange. I feel . . . it's happening to someone else. Oh, this is a course in sixth-grade philosophy. Someone else's left hand has just been cut off by a meteor. My left uniform sleeve has just automatically locked itself, sealed itself with self-sealant. I . . . (*Gasps.*) . . . lost some air, but the end of my wrist has frozen, frozen solid, scabbed itself with frost. (*Shuts eyes.*) Oh, *oh!*

HOLLIS (*concerned in spite of himself*)
Applegate!

APPLEGATE
Come help me, Captain!

HOLLIS
I wish . . .

APPLEGATE
Come help me, Captain!

HOLLIS
If I could . . .

APPLEGATE
Oh, sir, the irony. Telling you to come order me around ten minutes ago, and now *really* needing you. Oh, burn me, burn me to ashes, then burn the ashes to dust!

Radio sounds are heard. APPLEGATE begins to laugh quietly.

HOLLIS
What . . . ?

APPLEGATE (*stunned, amazed*)
Listen! You hear!? I . . . I'm in a meteor swarm, the very thing that cut off my hand is taking me with it, I'm being drawn away in space. Why, it's like being in a great big kaleidoscope. Those things, those toys, you held up to your eyes as a kid and looked in, and saw all the colors, shapes, sizes. A . . . a kaleidoscope. Look! Oh, beautiful. And taking me with it, me, *me*. . . . I don't deserve a trip like this. I never liked anything beautiful.

HOLLIS (*quietly*)
Never . . . ?

APPLEGATE
Well, maybe when I was young. (*A beat.*) Hear the *voices*?

The radio sounds are more than electronic static now, but are beginning to "talk," with small soft bursts of music, voices from another time, long gone, old radio broadcasts.

STONE
Voices?

LESPERE
Yes. (*Listens.*) Yes!

HOLLIS (*remembering something*)
No sound is ever lost.

APPLEGATE
What?

HOLLIS
Didn't we wonder, oh, years ago, what happened to sounds when they died, did they travel in space,

forever, living their own lives? Well, here's your answer.

LESPERE
What, an electronic cloud that—

STONE
Traps old radio broadcasts, news, music—

APPLEGATE
Yes!

They listen to CHURCHILL's VOICE in another year, talking out of World War II, and HITLER's VOICE raging and CROWDS shouting "Seig Heil" and ROOSEVELT's VOICE wandering in and out of hearing, and dance bands playing in 1930, 1955, 1974. . . .

APPLEGATE (*immensely touched and moved*)
Too much, too much. I'm the monster of all time,
and I go out like *this*. You stay behind and
die your plain vanilla deaths, and me, me, *me*?
I go out in style, in a swarm of meteors so
beautiful I can't move my tongue, and carried
along by the voices of Churchill and Hitler and
Roosevelt. Oh, friends! What *company!*

HOLLIS
Yes. . . .

APPLEGATE
Can you still *hear* me?

HOLLIS
Yes.

APPLEGATE
It's me and the whole grand bunch moving
out and around the worlds for the next ten
billion years. We'll be back, and Churchill will
still be talking, and Hitler will still be mad, and

Roosevelt will still be saying we have nothing to fear, nothing, nothing.

HOLLIS (*touched*)
So it finally happened.

APPLEGATE
Eh? What?

HOLLIS
It. The thing you were waiting for. *Something!*

APPLEGATE (*thinks; looks around; beams*)
Yes. . . . (*A beat.*) Yes! (*Nods wildly, happily.*) Yes! (*A long beat; then, slyly but warmly:*) So long. Burn, Captain, burn.

His light dims, fades, as does his voice.

APPLEGATE'S VOICE (*far away, happily fading*)
. . . Burn, burn . . .

The sounds of CROWDS, BANDS, VOICES, fade and vanish.

Faint electronic hums displace the above and fade into the background.

HOLLIS (*quietly*)
The same to you, Applegate.

LESPERE
Captain?

HOLLIS
Well?

LESPERE
Reception's fading for all of us. Why don't we get it over with and sign off?

HOLLIS
Good idea. Can you see the meteor swarm that took Applegate with it?

LESPERE
Oh, yes, yes, lovely. There . . . there.

HOLLIS
Can you see any of us?

LESPERE
No. . . .

HOLLIS
I can.

LESPERE
Impossible.

HOLLIS
But I see. Or *think* I see. There you go home in the dark, Lespere. And there you go off in the night, Stone. And, Barkley. (*Silence.*) Home *already?* (*A beat.*) Remember those summer nights when you were a kid and stayed out in the middle of the street playing ball until you couldn't see it was so dark, not wanting to go home, and at last all the mothers calling from blocks around, blowing whistles, yelling, and at last, dragging their bats, scuffing their shoes, all the boys went home, sad and hating it, as if summer would never come again, even though summer was the next night and the next after that?

LESPERE
I remember.

STONE
Keep *on* remembering. Don't let anybody say otherwise. Lespere, Captain? So long.

His light goes off.

HOLLIS
Sleep well.

LESPERE

Captain?

HOLLIS

Lespere?

LESPERE

Last one in's an old maid.

HOLLIS

Here goes nothing.

LESPERE

Nothing.

His light vanishes.

HOLLIS

Alone. There goes Woode toward the sun. There falls Stone near the Moon. There flies Barkley out beyond Mars and toward far Centauri, forever. There moves Applegate and his meteors and fine company of ancient men. Pieces of the kaleidoscope, all of us, but flying apart. And myself . . . alone. Add it up, Hollis. What did your life mean? More than Applegate's, less than Lespere's? Did you do one brief, bright, lovely thing that might be remembered for one astounding instant by someone somewhere sometime somehow? What, what did you *do*, Captain, that was worth noting, worth remembering, worth the softest breath to tell? (*Looks around.*) Just this: In a few hours, I'll hit Earth's atmosphere. When I do, I'll catch fire and burn like a meteor. I'll flash across the sky in flames. All the world will look up and see me for . . . three seconds . . . yes . . . three seconds. I wonder. . . . *Will* they look . . . *will* they *see?* (*A beat.*) Let's go . . . find, *out!*

The electronic sound has been building beneath his last few sentences. Now it rises to a crescendo, at the peak of which, eyes shut, his light goes out.

A beat. Then, across the darkness of the starred night, a burning light passes for a brief moment.

A BOY'S VOICE (*in darkness*)
Oh, look, there, look!

ANOTHER BOY'S VOICE
A falling star!

FIRST BOY'S VOICE
Make a wish!

SECOND BOY'S VOICE (*in quiet awe*)
Oh, yes. Make a *wish*. Make a wish!

A beat. Then all the stars go out.

The Foghorn

Curtain up.

A lighthouse tower. A late-middle-aged man, MC DUNN, crouched oiling some machinery in the darkening afternoon.

MC DUNN

There we are. Getting late. Sun'll be down in another half-hour. Fog's early. Here it comes. Welcome. (*He rises and casually salutes the mist.*) This place is yours. I live here by sufferance.

He rubs his hands and looks around.

MC DUNN

All right, McDunn. Everything shipshape? Lighthouse, light, and your own creature well-being? (*Flexes his arms.*) Ready for anything? Ready! (*Breathes deep.*) Ah, I *do* love this.

He goes to a circular rail and looks down.

MC DUNN

Damn me eyes, as the sailor-poets say. I'm really alone out here. No town for two hundred long miles that way north, no town for three hundred miles that way south, no town inland through that November mist for at least sixty fine lonely miles. There's just the empty coast, the empty roads, the empty land, the empty water, me, and one lone seagull, crying. All this considered, can I refuse the sea my love? I cannot. Why?

He lights his pipe, puffs, blows smoke.

MC DUNN

Because man is the Bored Animal. We need change. But where find it? (*Looks up.*) In clouds, as a boy, laid out studying the high atmospheres and symbolic configurations, the widenings and closures of pure air and white substance. Or in hearthfires, winter nights. Never two flames the same arabesque, baroque, rococo. Air and fire! But! But the sea, the ocean, beats both! More original than clouds, stranger than all hell's furnaces. It prowls a thousand shapes and colors, and no repeats in the billion years since the first tides rolled. Here's my sky and my hearth, full fathom five, all spread below, and no dull bored brute animal this. Go on, entertain me, that's it.

He freezes as he looks up and off.

MC DUNN

Hello, more entertainment! A motorboat. Why . . . that looks like Johnny's . . . No, is he *back* then? (*Squints.*) But, it is, it is! Hi, Johnny! Hi! (*Stops.*)He can't hear you. Well. Not alone. That's all right. Company. Someone real to talk at, so you don't run off the rail. Curious. I wonder has he heard the rumors? The old man's daft. He sees things by night. Worse, in raw noonlight. Can that be it? Let's tread easy and find out. John! Johnny! Hello! Tie on. Come up! You're just in time for the grand illumination!

He turns and busies himself with last-moment details, storing things in a kit, brushing the brasswork. He turns suddenly and looks around and down, listening.

MC DUNN

He's on the steps. Let's give him a great hullo! Eh?

He presses a button and there is one huge cry of the foghorn as JOHNNY steps to view, clapping his hands over his ears, beaming, panting.

JOHNNY
When, my breath! Those steps! I'm an old man!

MC DUNN
No, *I'm* old. You're young as the horses in the May fields! Johnny! It's good to see you!

He bear-hugs the young man, who smiles, then laughs.

JOHNNY
I'm crushed to bits! Angus! You look fine!

MC DUNN stands off and feels his own strength.

MC DUNN
Ah, it's from running up and down ten thousand steps a day! Johnny, it's great you're here.

JOHNNY
I thought I'd surprise you!

MC DUNN
Is that all it is—surprise?

JOHNNY
What else?

MC DUNN (*catches himself*)
Nothing. You've been off away?

JOHNNY
California!

MC DUNN
But you had to come back, eh? I mean, I hear they have a different ocean there, not half as much fun as this one? They have, I hear, second-rate hand-me-down fogs and fourth-rate hurricanes. You simply *had* to come home!

JOHNNY

Dear Angus, if you had a choice between a theater play, a new motion picture, or the view from this tower—

MC DUNN

I'd choose the tower's view, no argument.

JOHNNY

But, you have no relief! You're out here seven nights a week, three hundred and sixty-five nights a year. I don't think I've seen you on the mainland in years! You deserve—

MC DUNN

Or is "need" the word you're looking for?

JOHNNY

Deserve, need. Wouldn't you *like* to head for town a whole weekend?

MC DUNN

And drink and swarm myself with locust plagues of trouble? It sometimes flits across my eyeballs like a speck of licentious dust, but it goes if I blink. And who would sit in for me here tending the great babe in the night?

JOHNNY

Me.

MC DUNN

You!

JOHNNY

You raised me out here for two years when I was a kid, have you forgotten? You're next thing to my father. I worry—

MC DUNN

Why should you, unless someone has stuffed it in your left ear and pulled it out your right?

JOHNNY
Oh, Angus, there *is* talk. What's gone on since I left?

MC DUNN
It's not my doing. Ask the sea for answers. Johnny, I do *not* need relief, nor the town, nor drink. What's true is true. I *live* with reality, boy, at the foundation base of God's granite bulk himself. We came out of that sea a billion years ago, lost our gills, and put on manners, and things are still in that water which *do* rise up from time to time to frighten some and delight others. You've heard but the tail of the truth, and not the head and body.

JOHNNY
Fill in then, Angus. If I'm not to pile you in that boat and haul you back to the mainland, I got to have reasons to tell them there on the shore. Otherwise, they'll be out to relieve you of duty. Tell me everything.

MC DUNN
First let's check a few last things. The infernal night is on, and us not ready. There.

He tinkers some machinery in the great box at their feet.

JOHNNY
I'm waiting.

MC DUNN (*sighs*)
Well . . .

He looks down at the ocean.

MC DUNN
One night, two years ago, not long after you went away . . . Ah . . . you won't believe it.

JOHNNY
McDunn!

MC DUNN
All right . . . one night, I was alone. But aren't I always? One night alone here like Hamlet's father's dear ghost in the tower, I *felt* something. Maybe *heard* something with the fuzz inside my middle ear. . . . I woke from a sound sleep to come look down there at the waters of old time.

JOHNNY
And you saw . . . ?

MC DUNN
All the fish in the sea. All, every last one, they surfaced, they swam in billions, and lay out there, trembling, and staring up at the tower light going off, on, off, on, so I had swift flashes of their funny billion eyes. I turned *cold.* They were like a great peacock's tail out there, watching me, until midnight. Then, without so much as a sound, they slipped away, the billions of them was gone. I wonder . . . did they swim all those miles to worship? The light, the lighthouse, the tower high above the bleak waters, think how it must look and seem and be to the creatures, the dumb brutes there, the God-light flashing, and this tower declaring itself with its foghorn voice. They never came back, those fish, but don't you think for a while they thought they were in the Presence?

JOHNNY
They were, of a man with a wild tongue, and a taste for drink.

MC DUNN
I'm full, and the *sea*'s full.

JOHNNY
I can't tell that back on land, Angus! Come on, if we hurry—

MC DUNN
Hurry, hell, boy. The night is on us. It's too late.

JOHNNY
It's only two miles to shore!

MC DUNN
"Only" he says! Navigating in the dark, and the current gone wild in the last half-hour. No, boy, you'll stay the night, and float yourself in come dawn, God help you. For chances are you'll see tonight what I've seen and told no one of. Lend a hand, now. It's night, and fog, and much need of the light. There!

He turns a switch, and light comes on, turning behind them, misted, a shadowed motion of illumination.

MC DUNN
And now—the horn itself.

He touches a second button. The foghorn cries.

MC DUNN
Sounds like an animal, don't it? A big lonely animal set here on the edge of ten billion years calling out to the Deeps: I'm here . . . I'm here . . . I'm *here* . . .

The horn sounds again, not as loud.

JOHNNY
Angus . . .

MC DUNN
Say nothing, for it won't make sense. You *don't*

believe. But listen, Johnny, the foghorn calls, and the Deeps, they *do* answer. Why? Because one day years ago a man walked and stood in the sound of the ocean on a cold sunless shore and said, "We need a voice to call across waters and warn ships. *I'll make one*. I'll make a voice like all of time and all the fog that ever was. I'll make a voice that is like an empty bed beside you all night long, and like an empty house when you open the door, and like trees in autumn the first night the leaves have gone away. A sound like birds flying south, crying, and a sound like November wind and the sea on the hard, cold shore. I'll make a sound that's so alone that no one can miss it, and whoever hears will weep in their souls, and hearths will seem warm, and being inside best to all who hear in graveyard-distant towns. I'll make a sound and an apparatus to weep it with, and call it a Foghorn, and whoever hears it will know the sadness of eternity and the briefness of life."

The foghorn has blown at least three times, muted, during the above.

JOHNNY
Angus, you're right. The voice, just like you say. *You* might have invented it.

MC DUNN
Flattery will get you nothing, save more soliloquies. Listen.

They listen.

MC DUNN
That sound leads us the long way around to this night. We shall have a visitor! You'll *see!*

JOHNNY
Those billions of fish?

MC DUNN
No.

JOHNNY
One fish . . . a *whale* . . . ?

MC DUNN
Not a fish, and not a blood-warm mammal whale, but—Hist! Ah, yes! *There!*

He has come to the rim of the tower to peer out and point.

JOHNNY
Something . . . swimming toward our lighthouse . . . ?

MC DUNN
Aye.

JOHNNY
Something . . . big?

MC DUNN
"Tremendous" is nearer the mark.

MC DUNN lights his pipe and smokes, peering steadily. The foghorn blows, muted.

MC DUNN
It's a tide now, a motion to itself, hid down, and now rising, rising, a wave, a bubble, a bit of froth. Then, here, here, here it comes, boy.

JOHNNY
A head? A dark head? Eyes? One eye. Two? *Two!* And a neck, and more neck, and more—

MC DUNN (*mightily pleased*)
And *more* after that! Ten, twenty, thirty feet! And a body like an island of black coral and shells and crayfish, and all the subterrane. Ninety, one hundred feet in all! The monster! The beauty! It breaches! It breaches!

The foghorn cries!

The monster, in echo far off, cries.

MC DUNN
You *hear*?

JOHNNY
No.

MC DUNN
You *do!* Listen!

The monster cries, nearer.

JOHNNY
Impossible!

MC DUNN
No, we're impossible! It's merely fantastic. It's like *it* was ten million years ago. *It* hasn't changed. It's *us* and the land have changed, and gone impossible! *Us!*

The foghorn blows. The monster echoes, nearer.

JOHNNY
The light! Its eyes!

MC DUNN (*wonderfully enthused*)
Our own lighthouse beam flashed back from it in fine Morse code! And what does it *say*, Johnny?

JOHNNY
It's . . . a dinosaur?

MC DUNN
One of the tribe! And hear its lovely voice!

JOHNNY
But they died out!

MC DUNN
No, only hid away in the Deeps. Deep deep down in the deepest Deeps. Oh, hear the sound: Deeps. There's all the coldness and darkness and deepness in the world in words like that.

JOHNNY
What'll we do?

MC DUNN
Do? Why . . . enjoy the spectacle.

JOHNNY
It's circling around. Why? Why does it come here?

MC DUNN
Have you no ears?

The foghorn blows.

The monster cries.

MC DUNN
The foghorn *blows!* And the beast *answers!* There's a cry comes across a million years of water and mist. There's anguish that shudders the soul's marrow. Foghorn, monster cry, which is which? You might think that's another horn out there, lonely and vast and far away. The sound of isolation, a viewless sea, a cold night, apartness.

The monster cries.

JOHNNY
When did it first start coming here?

MC DUNN

Just a year ago. Think. Johnny, that monster lying far out, a thousand miles at sea and what . . . ? Twenty miles deep? Biding its time, maybe a million years old, this one beast, who can say? Not me. Think of it waiting a million years, could you wait that long? Maybe the last of its kind. And after all that waiting, here come men on the land and build a lighthouse and light a light and sound a horn and it cries out toward where you have been buried so deep the sound is no more than a whisper, an echo in your sleep, sea memories, no more, dim tides that remember a world where once you were young with thousands like yourself, all terrible beauties, but now you're alone, alone and no part of a world much changed.

The foghorn cries, muted. The monster cries, muted.

MC DUNN

But the sound of the foghorn comes and goes and you stir from the muddy bottom of the Deeps, and you move slow, slow, and your eyes open like the lenses of five-foot cameras and the furnace stokes in your belly and you begin to rise slow, slow. You feed yourself on great slakes of cod and minnow, on rivers of jellyfish, and pick your teeth with whales, and rise slow through the autumn months. You got to rise slow; if you surfaced at once you'd explode from the change in pressure. So it takes you months or years to surface, and then at last there you are, the biggest grand monster in creation, and here's the lighthouse calling to you with a long neck like your neck sticking way up out of the water, and a body like your body, and a voice like your voice!

The foghorn cries, faintly. The monster echoes.

JOHNNY

Oh, the lost thing. Has it waited that long? A million years, for someone to come who never came back?

MC DUNN

A million years. An insanity of time. While the skies cleared of reptile-birds and the swamps dried on the continental lands, the sloths and saber-tooths had their day and sank in tarpits, and men ran like white ants on the hills below Jerusalem. Last year, that creature swam round and round, round and round, all night. Not coming too near, puzzled. Afraid, too, maybe. And a bit angry after swimming all this way. But the next day, the fog lifted, the sun came out, and the beast swam away in the heat and silence and didn't come back. I suppose it's been brooding for a year now, thinking it over every which way. Maybe it only rises up once a year, on one night. I marked the date, anyway. And here it *is!*

JOHNNY

And coming closer!

MC DUNN

Blast if it isn't!

The foghorn cries. The monster cries.

JOHNNY

It's rising up! It's rising up! Gah! Its head is *level* with us!

MC DUNN

Stand back, boy!

JOHNNY

It's going to hit us! The light, Angus! The horn! IF we shut them off, it'll go away!

JOHNNY scrambles. The monster cries loud. The foghorn, in mid-shout, dies. The light goes out.

MC DUNN
Johnny, no! No!

The monster rages in fury.

MC DUNN
No. *That's* worst of all! It thinks we're gone! Switch on. Ah, quick! Switch on!

The light comes on. The foghorn blows.

There is an earthquake shudder, and the cry of the animal.

JOHNNY
It's fallen against the tower, it's grabbed hold, it'll break! We'll fall!

MC DUNN
Down the stairs! Below now! Quick!

JOHNNY
It's rising up again, up, up. No, no! So tall! Angus!

MC DUNN
Down! Down, you idiot!

MC DUNN pulls him. They drop through the stairwell.

A fierce green light shines upon the tower. Then . . . a shadow! And darkness. The crash of glass. The splintering of wood, metal, and stones. All falls to ruin.

Silence for a time; then the green light rises enough to find the two men sprawled flat, eyes tight, waiting. And above and around them an immense breathing and moaning.

JOHNNY
Angus?

MC DUNN
Alive. Thank God for this cellar. Listen. Sh. It's him, folded over and above us, not a stone's thickness away.

JOHNNY
The smell. It's terrible. I'll die.

MC DUNN
You'll live. But will *he?* Listen. The lament. The bewilderment. To him, the tower is gone. The light gone. The thing that called to him across a million years gone. So there's just him calling now, like the Foghorn come alive again, sending out great keenings, again, again. And ships at sea, passing late at night now, do they hear him cry and think: There it is, the lonely sound, the Lonesome Bay horn. All's well. We've rounded the cape. We're beyond the reef?

The gasping dies. The sound dies. There is a great tidal stir. We hear waves.

JOHNNY
Is he gone?

MC DUNN
He is.

They both sit up. The light begins to clear.

MC DUNN
Oh, wasn't that wonderful?

JOHNNY
Wonderful?

MC DUNN
And wasn't it sad?

They begin to get to their feet, and stop, for, far off, there is a cry.

JOHNNY
It's coming back!

MC DUNN
No. Going away. Going back to the Deeps. Having learned what? It doesn't pay to love anything too much in this wild, strange world? Or it's best to love anyway, even if it turns out to be no more than mere lighthouse, light, foghorn in a fog, and two mere anthill men in charge of it all?

JOHNNY
Do you think it knew what we were?

MC DUNN
As much as we know what *it* is; not much. Oh, Johnny, tomorrow get into the land, marry well, live in a warm house with bright windows and locked doors far away from the sea, come visit each year, but leave the ocean to me.

JOHNNY
It won't ever come back. I feel. It's gone back to wait another million years.

MC DUNN
Poor thing. Waiting out there. Waiting. Yes. While man comes and goes on this pitiful small world. Waiting . . . until . . . I rebuild this tower? And then, maybe . . . Johnny . . . if it *did* ever return? If the monster came to visit, and with its terrible sad voice reared up again to ask ancient questions?

We hear a lonely cry from far away.

MC DUNN (*slowly*)
To those questions, Johnny, what *answers* have you ready? What might you possibly . . . *say?*

They look at each other a long silent time, then look out steadily at the sea.

The light dims. The voice of the sea beast fades.

The curtain comes down.

ABOUT THE AUTHOR

RAY DOUGLAS BRADBURY was born in Waukegan, Illinois, in 1920. He graduated from a Los Angeles high school in 1938. His formal education ended there, but he furthered it by himself at night in the library and by day at his typewriter. He sold newspapers on Los Angeles street corners from 1938 to 1942—a modest beginning for a man whose name would one day be synonymous with the best in science fiction! Ray Bradbury sold his first science fiction short story in 1941, and his early reputation is based on stories published in the budding science fiction magazines of that time. His work was chosen for best American short story collections in 1946, 1948 and 1952. His awards include: The O'Henry Memorial Award, The Benjamin Franklin Award in 1954 and The Aviation-Space Writer's Association Award for best space article in an American magazine in 1967. Mr. Bradbury has written for television, radio, the theater and film, and he has been published in every major American magazine. Editions of his novels and shorter fiction span several continents and languages, and he has gained worldwide acceptance for his work. His titles include: *The Martian Chronicles, Dandelion Wine, I Sing the Body Electric, The Golden Apples of the Sun, A Medicine for Melancholy, The Wonderful Ice Cream Suit & Other Plays* and *The Illustrated Man.*